A Basketful

*Willow growing and Basket making
in Nottinghamshire and Lincolnshire*

Rodney Cousins

*This book is dedicated to Harry Summers of Sutton on Trent,
who inspired the research for this publication.
Also the many willow growers, workers and basket makers
who took the willow rod and created multi-use containers
for home, farm, factory, and even transport,
and gave the Trent Valley an international reputation
and products renowned for their quality*

A Basketful – Contents

Page	
2	Contents
3	Introduction
4	Trent Valley basketry willows
5 - 6	Willow Growers in Nottinghamshire and Lincolnshire
7 - 8	Willow growing and processing
9	William Scaling of Basford – Willow grower by Royal Appointment
10	A basket making apprenticeship, 1735
11	Francis Clark of Basford and Sutton on Trent – basket maker and rod merchant
12 - 13	Rod Peeling v. School
14 - 15	Rod Brakes and a French Stripper
16 - 17	John Marshall of Sutton on Trent – Buffing pioneer
18 - 19	Stripping, buffing and bolting the willows – photographs
20	Harrison's of Grantham – Willow Growers
21	Horace Mills of Newark – Willow Growers
22	Willow Holts in Nottinghamshire
23	The Osier Peelers
24	The Willow Works, Beckingham
25 - 26	Basket making tools
27	Basket making Workshop regulations, 1919
28	A Journeyman basket maker's list, Nottingham, 1872
29	Thomas Miller of Gainsborough – basket maker, poet and author
30	Lincolnshire basket making families – Wood and Ellmore
31 - 36	Harrison's of Grantham
37	Last of their line – Cyril Wakefield of Boston and Charlie Leggitt of Saxilby
38 - 40	Horace Mills of Southwell and Newark
41	The Beestons of Blyth
42	The Rawsons of Elston
43	Emile Janssens of Newark
44	Harry Summers of Sutton on Trent
45	The basket making migration to Sutton on Trent – the Taylors and John Olko
46	The Roulstones and Albert Newton of Basford
47 - 49	Basford, Nottingham – the nation's greatest basket making concentration
50 - 52	The East Leake basket making tradition, the Bramley's and the Mills dynasty
53 - 65	Lincolnshire basket makers from 1790 – 20th Century
66 - 77	Nottinghamshire basket makers from 1790 – 20th century
78 - 82	Basford basket makers 1861-91
83 - 86	East and West Leake basket makers 1841-1901
87 - 88	Sutton on Trent basket makers 1861-1901
89	Southwell 1891 – Horace Mills workers
90	A Willow timeline through Nottinghamshire and Lincolnshire
91	A basket making bibliography
92	Basket making terms
93 - 95	A Basketful – Place name index
96	Acknowledgements and basket making sources in Nottinghamshire and Lincolnshire
Inside back cover	Willow in the 21st Century
Back cover	The rod peelers saved for posterity

Introduction

> "...the valley of the Trent and its tributaries is the most important district in England, for both osier growing and basket making, not only for quality of output, but also quality of rods, and care given to their cultivation, and for the fineness of the basketry done there"
>
> Rural Industries Survey, Agricultural Research Institute, Oxford, 1926
> authors - FitzRandolph and Hay.

Less than a century later little remains of the once famous willow growing and basket making of this region. Hence the need for this publication, to put on record the willow growers and basket makers, who for centuries had their pride and skills woven in willow.

This study over thirty years, began with a project – "to record a local traditional country craftsman". The craftsman chosen was the late Harry Summers, basket maker of Sutton on Trent. Like many crafts the product looks simply made, but the eye and mind are deceived.

The craft required a long apprenticeship and many years experience, to turn the raw willow rod, into a functional container often combining strength with beauty.

So began an enjoyable trail through Libraries, Archives and Museums, but above all tracking down direct descendants of this once famous craft. Trade Directories dating back over two hundred years gave names and locations of the various makers and growers. Gradually the fascinating facts were uncovered, revealed and recorded for posterity.

The study covers the two historical counties of Nottinghamshire and Lincolnshire. From the Census returns 1841 – 1901, it is clear each county benefited from the other, sharing skills and expertise. Just over the border in Leicestershire, around Castle Donington, is another area with a rich basket making tradition and with Nottinghamshire connections, but sadly it must remain outside this publication.

The book may well have been called the 'World of Wicker', but in the end 'A Basketful' was chosen, and I hope you find an appreciation within its pages of the craft that brought an international reputation to the area, a great deal of employment, a vast array of products, but little wealth to the workers. A Basketful indeed!

822

| Seat 25 x 22in., 12/9. | Seat 30 x 23in., 18/- |
| „ 28 x 22in., 15/9. | „ 33 x 23in., 21/- |

Trent Valley Basketry Willows

Salix triandra – the almond leafed willow
One of the most common basketry willows, with varieties such as 'Whissenders', 'Pomeranian' (imported by William Scaling of Basford), 'Counsellor' (once popular in South Notts), 'Lincolnshire Dutch' (especially around the Gainsborough area), 'Black Holland', 'Mottled' or 'Black Spaniard'. 'Nottingham Spaniard', 'Rayn's Ten Feet' (from Castle Donington, Leics), 'Stone Rod', 'Glibskins', and the national favourite 'Black Maul'.

Salix viminalis – the Common Osier
The most common osier in willow holts, with basketry varieties such as 'Long Skin', and 'Brown Merrin' being the most popular in the Trent Valley. Other varieties included 'Mr. Kelham' originating from Bleasby, and 'Harrisoniana' originating, or in honour of Harrison's of Grantham.

Salix purpurea – the Purple Willow
With varieties 'Kecks' and 'Welch' being the most popular.

Salix daphnoides – the Violet Willow
Fairly rare, but was grown as a basketry willow around Beckingham, near Gainsborough.

Salix basfordiana – the Basford Willow
First observed about 1870 by William Scaling growing in his willow holt at Basford.

Salix sanguinea – the Belgian Red Willow
Introduced as a basketry willow by William Scaling from the Ardennes in 1863.

Salix decipiens – White Dutch, or Varnished Willow
Planted as a basketry willow, and observed at Cottam Willow holts by the Howitts.

Salix pentandra – Bay Willow
Planted as a basketry willow, seen at the former Lound Willow holt by the Howitts.

The above includes information kindly supplied by acknowledged willow experts, the late Mr. and Mrs Leiver Howitt of Farndon, authors of 'Flora of Nottinghamshire', 1963, and Mr. Ken Stott, former Willow Officer, University of Bristol, with extracts from Leicestershire grower, William P. Ellmore 'The Cultivation of Osiers and Willows', 1919.

"If the ground is in good condition two active boys will plant 4,000 cuttings per day" – quote by William Scaling in his 'Salix' notes 1871.

Willow Growers in Nottinghamshire and Lincolnshire

Sourced from Census Returns (C) and Trade Directories (D)
The birth years in the tables throughout the publication are approximate – Census source.

Name	Location	Birthplace	Year	Further information	Sources
Aldous Fred	Beckingham				1922 D
Andrew Wm Adkin	Boston,			BM & Rod dealer	1856 D
Barrick Ernest	Barrow on Humb.	Barrow	1865	Willow merchant	1892 - 1937 D
Barrick Jas & Sons	Barrow on Humb.	Barrow	1830	Willow dealers	1872/76 D
Barrick Thomas	Barrow on Humb.	Barrow	1797	Osier grower	1861 C
Barrick William	Barrow on Humb.	Barrow	1833	Willow Merchant	1885/9 D
Beeston Charles	Blyth	Worksop	1877		1908/22 D
Beeton Ernest	Barrow on Humb.			In business until 1920s	1920
Beeton John	Goxhill				1892 D
Beeton John W	Barrow on Humb.	Hull	1830	Willow grower	1877 -1905 D
Bettison William	Clarborough	Retford	1814	Willow merch/grower 16a @ Hayton	1860 NA &/81C
Bettison William	Retford		1777	Willow Merchant	1851 C
Birks Thomas	Lenton, Nottm	Lenton	1864		1900 D
Braisby Benjamin	Nottm	Leics, Wymeswold	1846		1893 D
Brearley Joseph	Crowland			Willow Merchant	1885 & 89 D
Brown Walter T	Bassingham	S. Carlton	1864	Willow Merchant	1909-1919 D
Clark Francis & Co	Sutton on Trent	Leics, Swithland	1843	13 acres (1911)	1900/08 D
Clarke Jas & Geo	Newark			Osier growers & rod merchant	1822 D
Cobb Fred	Sturton	Sturton le Steeple	1864		1908 D
Cobb James	Sturton	Sturton le Steeple	1820	38 acres	1881C & 1900 D
Cobham Robert	Farndon	Lancs, Mawdesley	1835	Rod Merchant	1881/91C & 1900 D
Darley John	Laneham	Laneham	1863		1881C '85/1900 D
Donner William	Barrow on Humb.			Willow Merchant	1885 & 89 D
Freeman Arthur	Sutton on Trent	Sutton on Trent	1870	Willow Merchant	1901 C
Freeman David	Sutton on Trent	East Markham	1838	Rod Merchant	1900/08 D
Freeman W	Sutton on Trent	Newton on Trent	1865		1900 D
Gale Herbert	Beckingham	Lancs, Bury	1882		1928/36/41 D
Gee Sarah	East Stoke	Elston	1797	Grower & osier dealer	1869 D
Gourley John	Beckingham			Willow grower	1908/22 D
Gourley John T	Torksey	Hardwick	1849		1881C & 1892 D
Greaves Benjamin	Cleethorpes				1885 & 89 D
Harrison W B & Son	Grantham	Grantham	1838	B Manuf & grower	1885 - 1909 D
Herrod Francis	Farndon	Farndon	1794	Osier grower/dealer	1848D 51/61C 69 D
Herrod Francis	Farndon	Farndon	1859		1881 C
Herrod Matthew	Farndon	Farndon	1836	140 acres, emp 1 man 2 boys	1881 C & '85/93 D
Herrod William	Farndon	Farndon	1819		1881 C
Hewitt Chas G	Gainsb, Lea Rd	Gainsborough.	1848	Farmer & willow grower	1881 C 1919 D
Lamb John	Bole			Willow grower	1908 D
Lamb John Sidsaph	Bole/Beckingham N.	Wheatley	1842	66 acres, empl 8	1881 C 1885/1908 D

Name	Location	Birthplace	Year	Further information	Sources
Lamb William	Grimsby			Willow Merchant	1889 D
Lucas Thomas	Milton	Milton	1857	Rod Merchant	1908 D
Marshall Thomas	Sutton on Trent	Sutton on Trent	1860	15a Carlton/20a Coll/5-10a Norm.on T	1891C
Marshall Frank	Sutton on Trent	Sutton on Trent	1886	Grandson of John, & son of Thomas	
Marshall John	Sutton on Trent	Sutton on Trent	1822	Farmer/willow Mercht. Buffing founder	
Mills John Horace	Southwell	East Leake	1856	7yr lease, 18ac willows	1890 NA
Mills John Horace	Newark	East Leake	1856	Holts @ Elston, Fiskerton, E.Stoke	
Parks Richard	Brocklesby	Market Rasen	1839		1881 C
Patrick Samuel	Lincoln, High St	Stamford	1820	Willow grower	1881 C
Pinder Wm Turner	Sutton on Trent	Laxton	1826		1881C '85 /1900 D
Platts W & Co	Beckingham			Willow grower	1908 D
Renwick E	Lound			Willow grower	1908/22 D
Richardson Rbt	Bingham	Bingham	1852		1893 D
Richmond John	Cromwell				1864 D
Royston Chas	Nottm	Leics	1835	Willow Merchant	1881 D
Scaling Wm	Basford	Yorks. Hull	1820	Grower/authority. Basfd 1852.400a.	1852 69 D 71C
Sharpe Wm	Grantham			Willow Merchant	1900 &1905 D
Smeeton Stephen	Carlton on Trent			Wand Holt, 3a	1663 NA
Smith Wm	Rolleston				1832 D
Stubbs Bros	North Cotes			Grower & Merchant	1930/37 D
Summers Thos	Sutton on Trent				1900/08 D
Templeman Thos	Norwell	Norwell	1822	Osier grower	1891 C 1900 D
Waine James	Nottm	Nottm	1846	Osier grower	1881 C
Wells Geo	Gainsborough	Tattershall	1835		1881C & 1892 D
Wilson Sons	Bassingham			Grower & Merchant	1900 D
Woodward Sarah A	Southwell			Willow grower	1922 - 36 D

Harvesting the Willow, Cowbit, Spalding c.1900

6   *A Basketful*

Willow growing and processing the rods

The willow rod is the basket maker's real 'flexible friend' – tough, responsive, quick growing and inexpensive, who could ask for more of a raw material? That was until a rival - cane - became readily available and along with plastic and cardboard replaced willow as the traditional container material. Before the replacement materials arrived, willow reigned supreme, and this area led the way. Let's follow the story…

The willow grower was required to grow several varieties to meet the basket makers' needs, i.e. from fine basketry to heavy duty hampers and skeps. The young willows known as 'sets' are cut from one or two year old rods into lengths of between 10-18" (25-46cm), depending on the variety. With spacing approximately 18" apart and between rows, it will result in about 20,000 sets needed per acre. The planting season is from November to March, with end February to March favoured. On good soil, the new plants require continual weeding to avoid suffocation and spoiling the growth. Each new set will produce up to ten shoots/rods in the first year, and with a ten acre site, the potential harvest could be 60 tons, or around 2 million rods.

Harvesting. Once October arrives and the leaves turn yellow and start to drop, it signals harvesting time. Rods required for 'buffing' are cut from November onwards, those for 'white' left until March, when the sap begins to move and making the removal of the skin (peeling/stripping) much easier. Until the 1950s the only tool used for harvesting was the rod hook (illustrated on page 25), cutting the rods individually. A truly back breaking job. A willow holt carefully and skilfully cut will produce for thirty years or more. Cut badly and the willow will die back and require replanting. The harvested willows are then taken to a yard for sorting, grading and tying into bundles known as 'bolts'.

Rod Processing. If white rods are needed, then the rods require stripping/peeling in the Spring as sap flow becomes active, and this task was traditionally mainly done by female seasonal labour, assisted by children, who should have sometimes been at school. The timing is critical and requires the rod's skin to be kept moist and avoiding a secondary skin growth. 'Couching' involves laying the willow rods on the ground in several layers, then covering with willow peelings to prevent the skin drying out. 'Pitting' is an alternative method in which the bundles/bolts are stood vertically in shallow running water, e.g. a stream. Both couching and pitting can extend the stripping/peeling period until around July.

Stripping the willow. To strip or peel the rods, hand brakes are used (illustrated on page 14). The individual rods are drawn through the brake, butt end first for about 6-8" (15-20cm), splitting the skin. The rod is then reversed, i.e. tip end first and the remainder of the rod is stripped, removing the skin and leaving a white rod. The lady strippers would be paid piece work which provided a welcome seasonal income, often with the help of children, to boost the output and earnings. Although rod peeling was considered below the status of domestic work, it did offer the opportunity of taking below school age children with them to work.

The Folk/Country dance connection – Strip the Willow. Romantic though it may seem, the willow strippers at the rod brakes did not perform any country dances. They were to busy earning a little extra income. However, I imagine the two lines in the dance representing the two iron jaws of the brake, with the couples dancing up to the end and peeling off, like the willow skin. Having tried both methods of 'stripping the willow' this is my interpretation, right or wrong.

Although all rod brakes serve the same purpose, designs do vary according to manufacturer's preference or the thickness of willow to be stripped. French peeling machines were trial tested in Somerset in the late 1920s, and such a model purchased by Harry Summers in 1947.

The machines greatly increased the output, but no doubt reduced the need for some of the seasonal workers. Whichever method is used for peeling, the rods must then be aired, by leaning them up outside to dry, to prevent mildew.

'Buff' willow is now the most popular finish for many basketry products. Few are aware that buff willow was first produced at Sutton on Trent, or how it was produced. See page 16 for this fascinating true story of Sutton on Trent's buffing and its 'liquid assets'. To produce buff willow by the present method, requires boiling the rods in their skins for several hours, often overnight, then peeling them with rod brakes. Women stood on either side of the boiling tank, with each worker stripping up to 1½ tons of willow rods per day. The sweet smell and steam brings back vivid memories to all those who have experienced buffing. After stripping the rods, as with the white rod production, they require careful drying outdoors to prevent mildew and discolouration. Not all willow varieties produce good buff rods.

'Brown' Rods are neither boiled or stripped, but retained in their skin as a natural preservative and generally used for basketry used outdoors, such as agricultural baskets, fences/hurdles and fish traps. Brown rods command a lower price than white or buff as they require less processing and often contain forked or inferior rods.

Once the willows are processed, into white, buff or brown rods, they are then sorted into bundles/bolts, consisting of rods of the same length, then tied using a willow rod. This process known as 'bolting' is illustrated on page 19. The bolts, however, historically varied in size, but now are commonly sold by weight.

The main willow growing and basket making area today in the UK is Somerset. The 'withy beds' as they are known, along with the basket making workshops are very much part of their cultural heritage. The willow story can be seen from start to finish, from withy bed to workshop, from worker to basketry for sale. Thousands of visitors experience willow first hand and I hope appreciate the skills involved to produce what was once a world of wicker.

Painting 'Wickerwork' by W Hallam Pegg, exhibited at the Royal Academy, 1943 and features the Beehive Works, East Leake.

William Scaling of Basford
Willow grower by Royal Appointment

Born in Hull about 1820, William moved to Edinburgh by the 1840s as a basket maker and, by 1852 to Basford. The previous year he was awarded a medal at the Great Exhibition and retained royal patronage from Queen Victoria for the next ten years. There are claims that in the 1850s, William Scaling had 400 acres under willow cultivation in Basford, Colwick and Toton, and employed some 200 workers. However there is no doubt, William Scaling should be credited for putting Basford on the map, with regards willow growing and perambulator and wicker furniture making and patenting a device for splitting willows.

In the 1861 Census, William is listed as a widower, employing 27 men, 26 boys and 27 girls, plus no doubt additional seasonal workers, making him one of the largest UK employers in the willow industry at that time. In 1871, he had remarried, to a Basford girl, had a son William aged 5, and switched almost entirely to willow growing with 100 acres and employing just 8.

A copy of a publication by William Scaling in 1871, is in the Local Studies Library, Nottingham. In the book, Scaling estimated between 6,500-7,000 acres of willow were under cultivation in the UK, but in 1866 still imported 4,400 tons from France, Belgium, Netherlands and Prussia. Scaling had over 300 varieties of basketry willow at Basford and discovered a variety which he named Salix frigilis basfordiana.

William stated "that if the ground is in good condition, two active boys will plant 4,000 cuttings per day". He also quoted "it is now greatly the fashion to make baskets of willows peeled by steaming or boiling, instead of peeling by the ordinary cause (white)...and in the process of boiling, the colouring matter contained in the bark stains the willow a buff colour. The extra durability of baskets made of the boiled willows, over those made of willow peeled white only require to be more widely known to make white baskets things of the past." He also states "the best and finest willows in the kingdom are grown in the county of Nottingham, and they always realise a higher price than any others, either home or foreign growth".

In the 1881 Census, Scaling is described as Perambulator Manufacturer employing 6 men. William died in January 1887 and in 1891, his son William was listed as an Employer Basket maker, but by 1901 had moved up to Lancashire as a book keeper with his wife and son, William.

The Nottinghamshire Conservation Society planted a small bed of Basford willows beside the River Leen at Basford in 1985 as a living reminder to William Scaling, a great among the nation's leading willow growers.

An apprenticeship agreement to a Stamford basket maker, 1735

This indenture made the **twenty fourth** day of **July** in the **ninth** year of the reign of our Sovereign Lord **George the Second** by the Grace of God, of Great Britain, (France) and Ireland. King Defender of the Faith, and so forth. And in the year of our Lord **One thousand seven hundred and thirty five**. Witnesseth, that **Richard Gargrave & Robert** ..... Churchwardens of the parish of **St John** in the Borough of **Stamford** aforesaid. And **Richard Law & Francis Sidney** Overseers of the Poor of the said Parish, by and with the consent of His Majesty's Justices of the Peace for the said Borough whose names are hereunto described, have put and placed, and by these presents to put and place **John Lion of the age of thirteen years** a poor child of the said Parish, apprentice to **John Lyon the elder of Stamford, aforesaid, Basket maker** with him to dwell and serve from the day and dates of these presents, until the said Apprentice shall accomplish his full age of **twenty one years** according to the Statute in that case made and provided: During all which term, the said Apprentice his said Master faithfully shall serve in all lawful business, according to his power, wit, and ability, and honestly, orderly and obediently in all things demean and behave himself towards his said Master and all his, during the said term. And the said for himself, his Executors and Administrators, doth Covenant and Grant to and with the Churchwardens and Overseers, and every of them, their and every of the Executors and Administrators, and their and every of their Successors for the time being, by these presents, that the said John Lyon the said Apprentice in **the Art of Basket maker, shall teach and instruct**. And shall and will, during all the term aforesaid, find, provide and allow unto the said Apprentice, meet, competent, and sufficient Meat, Drink and Apparel, Lodging, Washing and all other things necessary and fit for an Apprentice. And also shall and will provide for the said Apprentice, that he be not any way a Charge to the Parish, or Parishioners of the same: but of and from all Charge shall and will have the said Parish and Parishioners harmless and indemnified during the said term. And at the end of the said term, shall and will make, provide, allow and deliver unto the said Apprentice double Apparel of all sorts, good and new, (that is to say) a good new Suit for the Holy Days, and another for the Working Days. In Witness whereof, the parties above said to the Presents Indentures interchangeably have put their hands and seals the Day and year above written.

(Signatures or their marks and seals)

Transcript from the original in the collection of Lincolnshire Archives – Ref 13/2/5 – Stamford St John Parish. 1735

Francis Clark – basket maker and rod merchant
Basford and Sutton on Trent

Francis was born in Swithland Leicestershire in 1842 – his father James was a butcher and his mother Mary (Rayns of Kegworth) was from a basket making family. By 1871 he had married Elizabeth from Billesdon, Leicestershire, and had a daughter Laura, born in Radford, Nottingham. In 1874 his eldest son, Ernest Francis was born in Basford, followed by another son and two daughters – gleaned from the 1881 census, when Francis was listed as a basket maker in West Gate. By 1891 he had moved to a factory in Chelmsford Road, with eldest daughter Laura also listed as a basket maker. In 1900 Francis had moved to Sutton on Trent and established a buffing factory on Grassthorpe Road (the factory buildings still exist as part of Walton's site). Meanwhile Francis's son Roland continued as Clark & Co on Chelmsford Road, and is listed in the 1901 Census with his mother and four brothers and sisters. Roland was recorded as a Wicker Furniture Manufacturer, and later listed in the 1908 Kelly's Trade Directory.

The rod factory at Sutton on Trent and Osier beds were advertised for sale in the, 8th February, 1911 edition of the Newark Advertiser. "Two storey factory 45' X 24', with large store room 24' X 44', and two Rod Boilers, and sheds at rear. Stables for 4, Harness Room, Chamber over, Cow sheds, Piggeries, Crew yard. Paddock 85 on OS map, Grassthorpe Road. Lot 2 Osier Holt known as 'Moor Leys', Bulham Lane, 3½ acres of Black Moles (Mauls), all young stools in good condition. Lot 4 'Trent Holt', 10 acres, adjacent to River Trent. Whole property in occupation of Mr. Francis Clark" (then 69 years of age)

Sutton on Trent - Clark's Buffing factory, Grassthorpe Road. Photo 1997

A Basketful

Rod Peeling v. School

From Nottinghamshire School Log Books it is clear that good school attendances depended on no other demand from the farm or the willow harvest.

Norwell Charity School, 4 April 1844 – Meeting of the Trustees "...it was agreed that the holidays should be made to fall in with the seasons when the children are wanted for work, as far as can be done...harvest, rod peeling, and a short vacation for Christmas". Things had not improved by 1880 when the schoolmaster wrote to the Vicar "to keep the school open during rod peeling, and not to have any holiday". But the authority seemed to fighting a losing battle. In 1893 "school closed for two weeks - rod peeling". In 1904 the Easter holidays were postponed to suit rod peeling.

Caunton School, 25 April 1870 ..."small attendance owing to rod peeling." 2 May ... "still very low owing to rod peeling". 9 May ..."low attendance owing to rod peeling and cowslip gathering". Further absences were June "tenting cherries"(bird scaring), July "'pea pulling", late July "harvesting", September "still gleaning" followed by "Cricket match and blackberry season", late September. The following year, almost as bad with February "bean dropping", and full circle 17 April "rod peeling not yet finished". 1 May,- "six children return after three weeks rod peeling". 1872 -78 similar pattern. 25 April reads "about twenty children go to work in the rod yards". 1880 – 93 similar entries. Followed by 1894, 13 April "school closed for two weeks – rod peeling" 3 May "rod peeling not yet finished". 1895 – 97 school closed for four weeks each April. Up to 1918 two or three weeks holiday each April "rodding". Until finally from 1919 onwards the rodding entries cease.

East Leake meanwhile experienced similar problems. April 1876 "great falling off in attendance, many children employed peeling osier rods".

Farndon - April 1867, "small attendance, commencement of peeling osiers in village'. "April 1879,"not half of children present this week owing to holting".

Elston – similar pattern. 1865 "thin attendance, absentees at the osier ground and bird tenting".

For a while the schools grudgingly did 'spare the rod' after all.

Former Rod Peeling yard and storage barn of Herrods, willow growers. Main Street, Farndon.
Photo: picturethepast,
Reg Baker 1979

12   A Basketful

Rod Peeling v. School in focus

Spalding area. Possibly Cowbit. All hands enlisted for peeling c.1900. Note the stripped willow in the background.

Also in the Spalding area. Basket Maker Thomas Aistrup had osier beds in the area about 1900. Note the youngsters on the learning curve, but should they be at school?
Both Spalding photos via M.Elsden.

Rod peelers at Bole, near Retford. Child labour much in evidence. Is it a 'rustic scene' or strip the willow for extra pennies. Photograph taken around 1900 by local photographer Edgar Welchman. His fine collection is in Retford Museum.

A Basketful   13

Basket making tools – Rod brakes

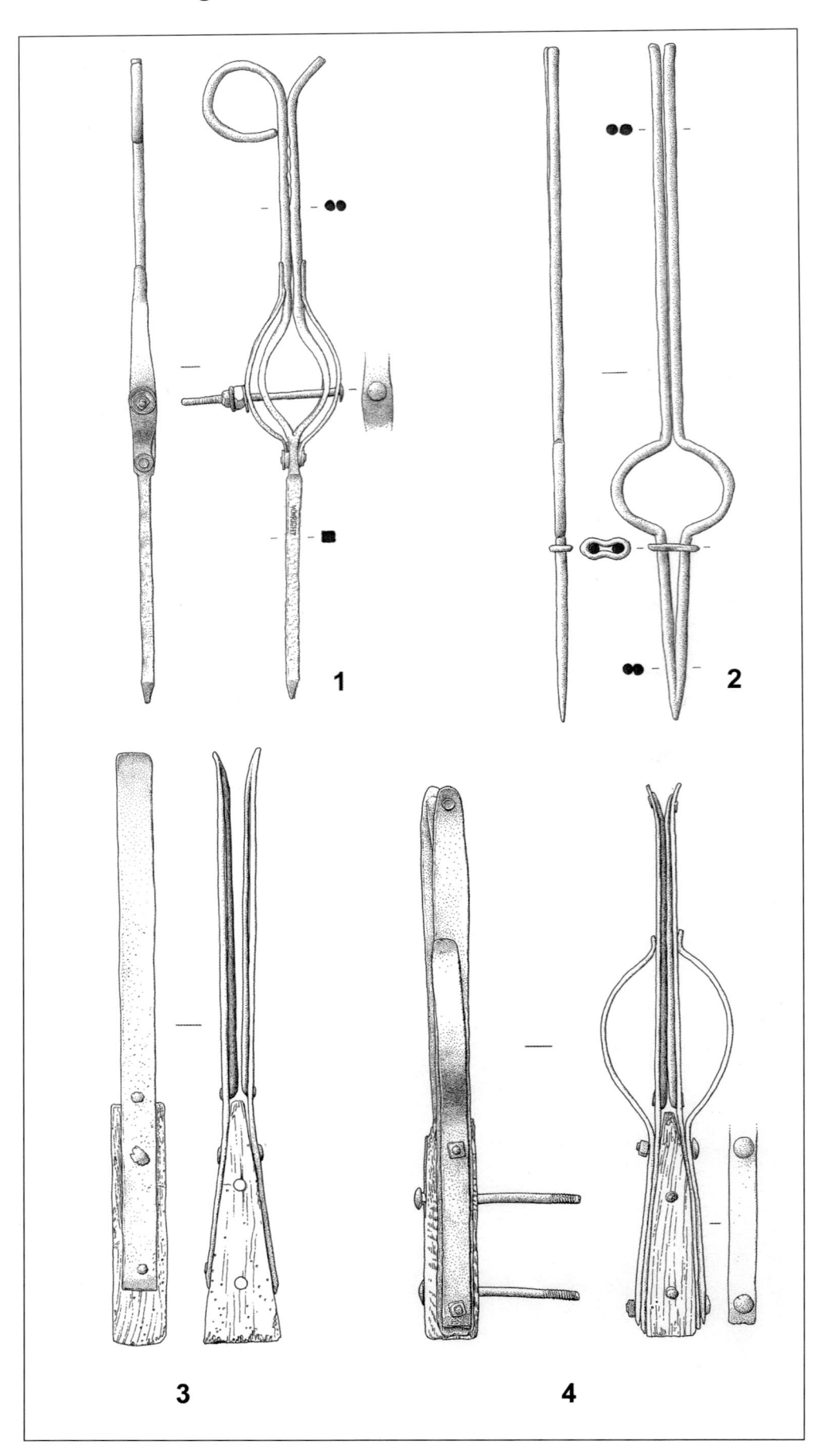

Four examples of Rod brakes, 70-79 cm in height, used for stripping the willow, at Mills of Newark.

Drawings by David Hopkins, Heritage Lincolnshire.

14   A Basketful

A French Stripper

New Device for Old Industry.

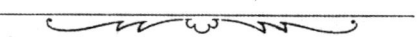

Willow Peeling Machine

Rouy & Masson's Patent.

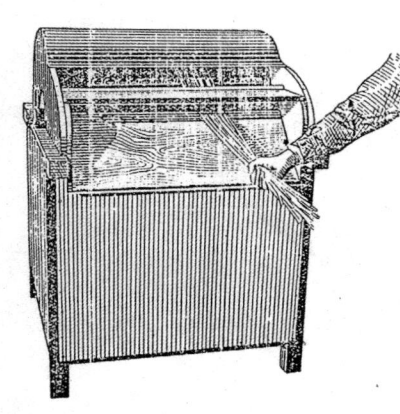

AWARDS.

1928. Silver Medal Agricultural Meeting of Badonviller.
1929. Silver Medal Willow Growers' Trade Committee.
1929. Silver Medal Ministry of Agriculture

By using this machine, the gloss is preserved, the tops are not cut nor the rods crushed.

It is the strongest made, all pieces of special steel, is proof against wear.

It is the simplest, it does not need any adjusting, this being done once for all at the factory.

It is the most practical because you can peel rods from 1 to 10 feet long.

There is no maintenance, only two bearings to be oiled.

The output is considerable.

With the smaller model for one man (model No. 1) you can peel 20 cwt. of rough middle size willows in 8 hours.

With model No. 2 for two men, you can peel 40 cwt. in the same time.

It is a really economical machine, a 1½ B.H.P. engine for the smaller model, and a 3 B.H.P. engine for the larger model is sufficient.

Advert c.1930

The next page of this advert reads and claims – " All Willow Growers will be interested in this machine. The principle of working is exactly the same as by hand stripping only the old trouble of splitting or crushing the rods has now been completely overcome by this machine. A 13 year old boy can easily work it. Instead of one rod being peeled at a time, bunches of from 30 to 150 rods are made 'white'. The willows are absolutely 'White' and you will always get a perfect gloss. Speed approximately 260 r.p.m. Prices: No1 Machine £29.0.0. Machine No2 £38.0.0. Sole Distributors for the British Isles – Hawkes & Sons Ltd, Agricultural Engineers, Taunton."

Imagine my surprise to find one such machine outside Harry Summers workshop, in the 1970s. With Harry's permission I contacted the local newspaper, hoping someone would have vivid recollections and perhaps resentment of 'the machine' replacing people. One evening a photo and article appeared – another surprise. The headline read "On show a French Stripper aged 24…and it's all in the cause of education and knowledge". The photo showed me and the Stripper. No offers followed of information or otherwise!

John Marshall of Sutton on Trent – Buffing Pioneer

Sutton born, in 1822, John Marshall was a farmer of 60 acres. According to the 1861 census, he employed 2 labourers and a boy. Ten years later, he was described as a Master Basket maker employing 11 men and 2 labourers. What led to this change and rapid increase in labour is worthy of further investigation.

Local tradition has it that John Marshall employed a travelling basket maker, William Chapman from Lincoln. Chapman harvested Marshall's crop of Trent-side willows and converted them into much needed containers. It quickly developed, supplying both local and needs further afield. The chance discovery that some of the stored willows produced a golden brown rod when stripped led to a sudden national demand. However the reason for the colouration was somewhat of a mystery.

In the willow processing, to keep the willows 'live' to enable stripping, i.e. removal of the skin, it is essential the rods are regularly watered, or stood vertically in streams. Workers apparently found their own method, a natural process in the course of the working day, by relieving themselves on the stored bundles of willow. Such was the demand for buff willow, that additional supplies of the natural additive were required in large quantities. A lucrative trade with the villagers, involved the collecting of buckets of urine for a few pennies. (A pint of beer or a loaf cost a penny). The bundles of rods were boiled in the 'liquid', then stripped, resulting in 'buff' willows.

It was gradually realized that less 'additive' was required, and indeed pure water produced the same result. The dye was naturally in the willow skin. However, full credit should be given to John Marshall and Sutton on Trent for the process of 'buffing' to the world of wicker!

Within a few years, a factory was established to process buff willows employing over 40 for this task alone. The factory, for obvious reasons situated on the outskirts of the village on Grassthorpe Road is still in use, although for a different purpose. The buffing process was discovered in 1867 and the following Census of 1871 makes interesting reading, with now 27 basket makers in the village. Eighteen of them non-local, coming from such places as London, Ireland, Hull, Manchester, Ormskirk and even Pittsburgh USA. Sutton on Trent experienced industrial espionage on a grand scale, and soon the secret was out and buffing became universal.

John Marshall's son Thomas, then his son Frank, continued the business until 1946. For a while Frank was also employed by the local authority as a Basket Making Instructor for schools and Adult Education. The family used home grown willows, having about 40 acres under cultivation at nearby Carlton on Trent, Collingham and Normanton on Trent. To collect the Collingham willow crop, an empty horse and cart was ferried across the River Trent and returned fully loaded. It must have been a strange sight, but for the locals it was all in a day's work.

Marshall's of Sutton on Trent

Frank Marshall, 1960

> "It is now greatly the fashion to make baskets of willows peeled by steaming or boiling,
> instead of peeling the ordinary course (white),
> ...and in the process of boiling, the colouring matter contained in the bark stains the willow, a buff colour.
> The extra durability of baskets made of boiled willows, over those
> made of white peeled willow, only requires to be more widely known
> to make white baskets things of the past" – William Scaling, 1871.

Stripping and Buffing

Willow stripping group at Fiskerton, Newark. In the 1890s Horace Mills had over 40 acres of willows at Southwell and Fiskerton employing 39 seasonal peelers listed in the 1891 Census.
Photo: Newark Museum

Calverton area, taken by local photographer John Scott, about 1900. Photo: Burton Joyce Local History Society.

Buffing the willows at Horace Mills factory, Farndon Road, Newark, 1928. Eight workers are shown stripping the rods amid the steam after several hours boiling. Photo: Newark Library, Local Studies

Mrs F. Moore of Newark recalls –
"…after boiling willows overnight, women arriving in the morning, would stand on planks, and pulled the willow to the side [of the boiling tank] with iron hooks. Then they stripped off the peel, while the willow was very hot. The only protection the women had was old rags, wrapped around their fingers. The shed smelt from the damp warm bark".

18   *A Basketful*

Bolting the Willow

Series of photographs from the Spalding area, c.1900. Possibly at Thomas Aistrup's Yard at Cowbit.

The photographs show the sequence of sorting, grading and bundling (bolting) the white rods, which have previously been stripped. The bolts are made to a specific weight, irrespective of the length of the rods, for storage or transit. Photos: Michael Elsden

Notice a bat being used to get all the thick ends (butts) level. An example of a Bolting bat was found at Bassingham, and stamped 'W&S', representing the Lincoln growers and basket makers, Wright & Son, who had willow holts in the village.

A Basketful

Harrison's of Grantham

Horse and cart loaded with freshly harvested 'green' willows at Dry Doddington, bound for Grantham for sorting and processing. Photo: Grantham Library.

Harrison's yard, Dysart Road, c.1890. Here the rods were graded and stripped for white or buffed willow. During May 1901, a serious fire destroyed a large quantity of stored rods, resulting in a shortage at the workshops, causing many workers to be laid off for several weeks. Photo: Grantham Library.

Woman scalded to death in cane factory accident

A FIFTY-two-year-old woman died after falling into a copper of boiling water at work.

Eliza Moulds was working at Harrison's osier rod yard, Barrowby Road, dragging bundles of rods from the coppers.

Julia Morris told an inquest Mrs Moulds was trying to disentangle two bundles of osier canes at the bottom of the copper, when she slipped and finished up to her knees in scalding water.

Both women had been standing on a 12 inch brick wall which was there to stop them falling in.

Workmate Caroline Deacon said there was a man whose job it was to untangle canes but the women would not ask him.

"He has refused to on previous occasions," she said. "He was a very stupid man and would not do work when it is wanted.

"He was sitting on the edge of the copper while the women were at work."

Dr Wilson, the surgeon, said the woman died of exhaustion arising from the scalds.

"The water must have been boiling to have caused such scalds," he said.

The jury returned a verdict of death by accidental scalding.

A report from the Grantham Journal, 1872. The fatality happened during the buffing process, and within a few years of its discovery at Sutton on Trent. By 1881 W.B. Harrison was one of the largest willow growing and basket making firms in the UK. - 1881 Census. Article from Grantham in the News by J.R. Pinchbeck.

Horace Mills of Newark

Advert appearing in W.J. Cook's Newark Trade Directory, 1897-8. At this time Mills was in the process of transferring his business from Southwell to Newark and by the early 1900s was employing nearly 300 workers.

Photograph from a press article about the firm in 1926 which shows workers near the Farndon Road factory. Note the tent-like structure on the left, for storing the willows prior to peeling.

Advert from the Newark Herald, 2nd November, 1918 with an interesting distinction between women and girls.

A Basketful   21

Willow Holts in Nottinghamshire

The Trent flood plain around Gainsborough was the most productive area in the UK for willow growing.

1880s The main areas of willow growing and acreage in Nottinghamshire

West Burton	108.9	Beckingham	70.2	Bole	50.6	Southwell	48.4
Dunham	39.0	Farndon	37.4	Shelford	35.7	Rampton	33.8
Rolleston	33.8	Balderton	25.6	East Stoke	23.0	Cromwell	22.4
Norwell	21.2	Chilwell	20.4	Sutton on Trent	20.3	Toton	18.1
Fiskerton	16.8	Colwick	16.8	Lound	16.5	Thorpe	16.5
Gonalston	16.1	East Leake	14.2	Bingham	13.6	Basford	12.5

Total 945.6 acres
Sourced from 25" OS maps and researched by Corinne E. Phillips, author, 'Skeps and Scuttles'.

1917. Acreage for basketry willows – Nottinghamshire 720 acres, Leicestershire 2-300, Lincolnshire about 200 (mainly Gainsborough area). Then next in importance Somerset, then Thames Valley, Cambridgeshire & Huntingdon - FitzRandolph and Hay Survey 1926.

1944. Land Utilisation Survey – Part 60 Nottinghamshire – approximate willow acreage.

Cottam/S.Leverton	30	Beckingham	21	Bole	21	West Burton	15
Fiskerton	10	Lound	8	W.Retford	6	Blyth	5
N.Leverton	5	Carlton on Trent	5	Sutton on Trent	4	East Stoke	2
Upton (by Southwell)	1	Sturton le Steeple	1	Norwell	1		

Total 158 acres

> "Willow growing areas of Nottinghamshire and Leicestershire is the most important…the standard of cultivation there (Trent Valley) is above that of any other District"
> Rural Industries Survey, Agricultural Institute, Oxford – FitzRandolph and Hay, 1926.

Willow in verse
'Near the Garrick milestone
Nothing there grew beneath the sky
But willow scarcely 6' high
Or Osiers barely 3' dry,
And there of only one years crop
The flood did fairly overtop'

By John Taylor, 1580-1654, known as the Water Poet.
(The Garrick stone is in the parish of Heckington).

The Osier Peelers

S WILLIAMS

'The Osier Peelers'
And when moist April comes in tender green,
The villagers in osier grounds are seen,
Peeling the tapering wands; and all day long
Is heard the merry tale and rustic song;
For 'tis the earliest harvest of the year,
Commenced before the cuckoo doth appear.

"Osier cutting is the hardest work – stooping from morning until night, and bending down the tall headed willows with one hand, whilst the other wields the ponderous and sharp edged hook. When the harvest is completed, the last rod is decorated with ribbons, and then on to a Osier Feast Supper...with food, games, tales and songs"

From 'Pictures from Country Life', 1847 and 'Hawthorndale Village Revisited' 1857, both by Thomas Miller, Gainsborough born author, poet and basket maker.

A Basketful

The Willow Works, Beckingham

A rare survival of a purpose built Willow Works, c.1890. This recently restored building was for the grading and storing of willows. A further workshop behind, now demolished, was used for stripping and buffing the rods. The Willow Works are part of a Heritage Lottery Project to preserve the building, establish an Interpretive Centre and to develop the natural and educational potential of the associated marshes. Shown below is a sketch of the complex as recalled by local resident Fred Gosling. Photo and information via Mrs Freda Proudley, Beckingham Local History Society.

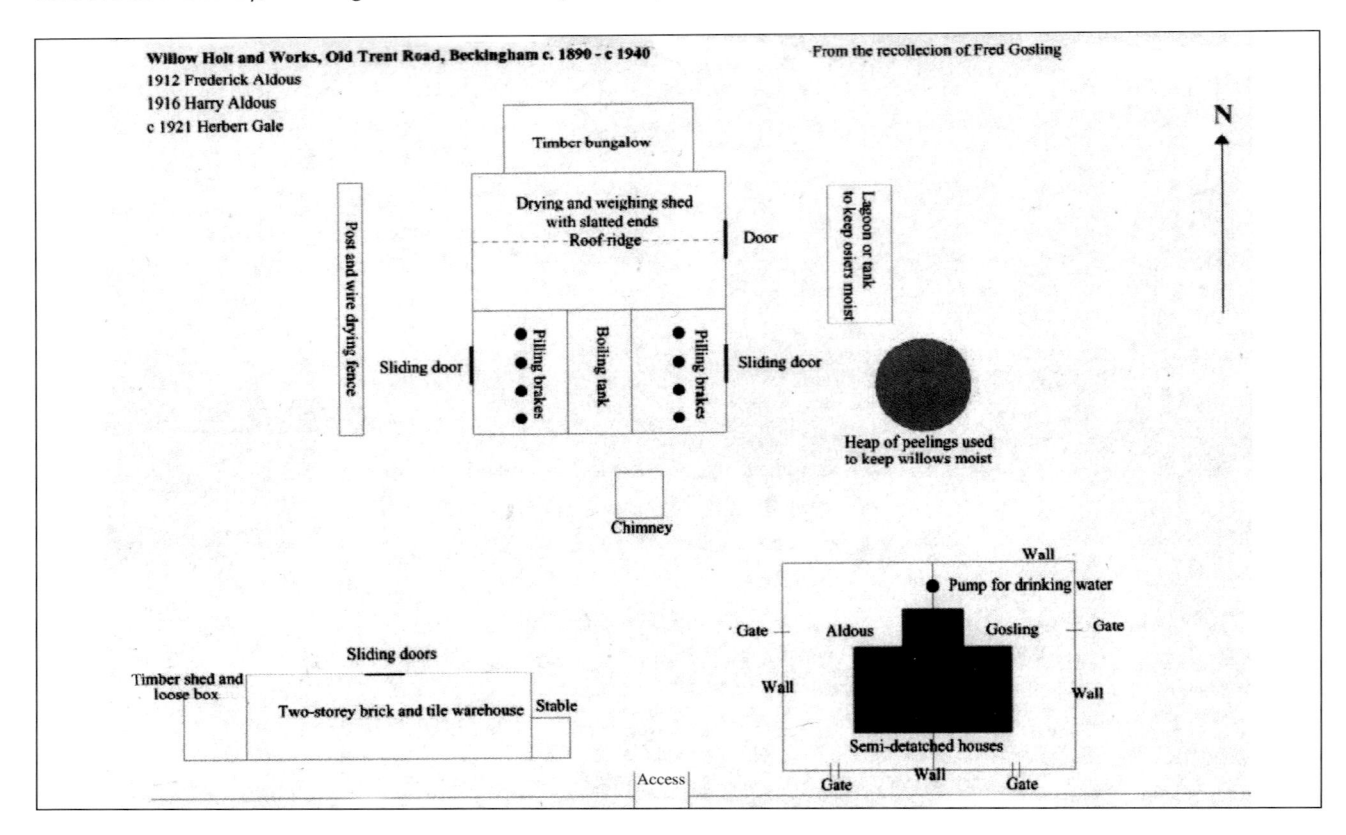

Basket making tools -1

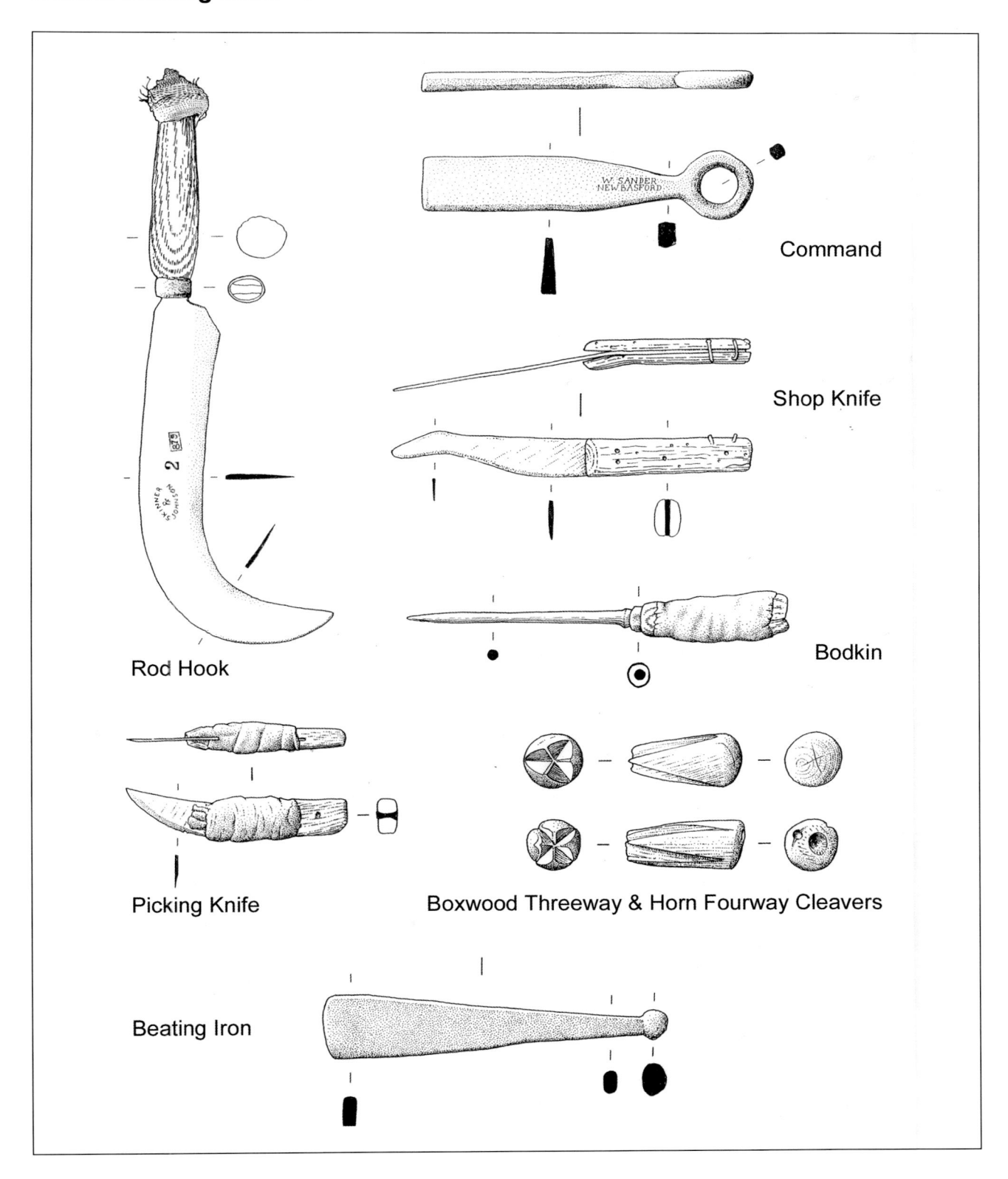

Command

Shop Knife

Bodkin

Rod Hook

Picking Knife

Boxwood Threeway & Horn Fourway Cleavers

Beating Iron

Rod harvesting hook used by Charlie Leggitt of Saxilby. Cleavers from Harry Summers and the remainder from Horace Mills of Newark. Drawing by David Hopkins, Heritage Lincolnshire.

A Basketful

Basket making tools – 2

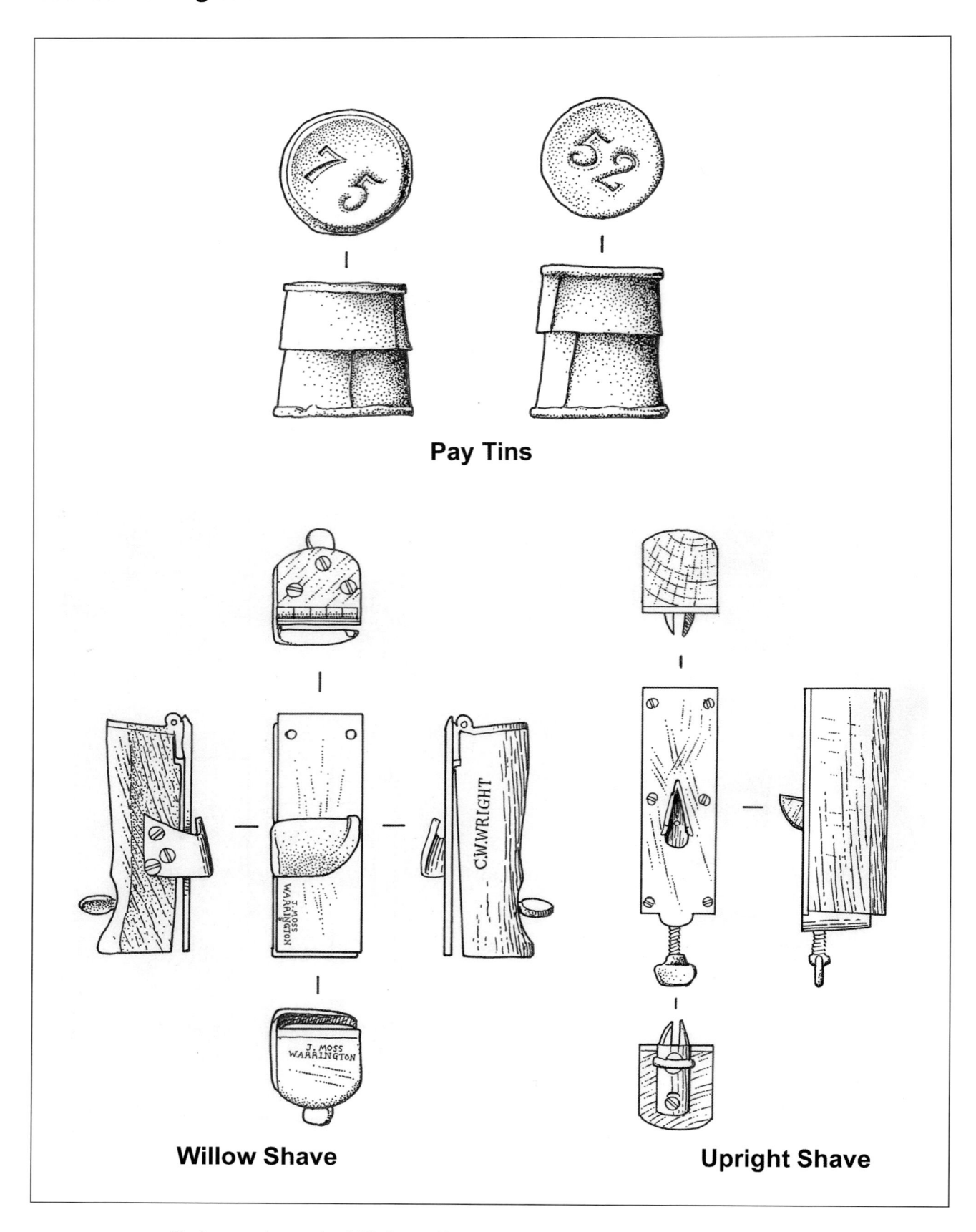

Pay Tins

Willow Shave

Upright Shave

Tinplate pay tins used at Mills factory Newark, with employee's number stamped on the top. Below - two shaves used by Harry Summers for skein (split willow) work and formerly used at Wright & Son, Basket Makers of Lincoln. Drawings by David Hopkins, Heritage Lincolnshire.

Rules, Regulations and Working Conditions for the Basket Making Industry Agreed to by the Interim Industrial Reconstruction Committee and to operate from December 1st 1919

Working Hours – Each district to have the option of arranging their own working times…so long as the total does not exceed 48 hours per week (excl of one hour for lunch).
Overtime – No overtime whatever to be permitted.

Apprentice Laws & Rules (Boys) –All apprentices to be properly bound before they reach the age of 16 and 3 months, and not to work on the plank more than 3 months before being properly indentured. Standard indenture form to be adopted…duly witnessed by the General Secretary of the Employers' & Employees Assoc, or any person duly authorised by them.

Number of apprentices allowed – Any employer may have one apprentice. If he employs 5 men on average for 2 years - 2 apprentices, 10 men - 3 apprentices, 17 men - 4 apprentices; 25 men - 5 apprentices. If employer has more than 25, he may have one apprentice for every 5 men.

Instructor's Remuneration – The apprentice must be placed in the charge of a skilled employer or workman for instruction. When piece rates are paid, the instructor to be paid for their joint efforts. The instructor agrees to make the employer an allowance for the use of the apprentice. Where the instructor is paid time rate, the employer takes all the work produced by the joint efforts of the instructor and apprentice.

Apprentices' Remuneration The employer pays the apprentice in all cases at the following scale: 1st year ….. 2nd yr ….. per week, plus the same bonus that the workman receives. (Figures left to each Association for decision).

Instructors' Responsibility – No instructor shall have in his charge more than 5 apprentices at the same time, or take an apprentice to instruct for less than 2½ years.

Employers' Responsibility - …to see his training is completed, until he reaches the age of 21 years. The apprentice must serve his full term of apprenticeship in the employer's workshop.

Employers' Sons, Employers' and Instructors' Responsibility, & Penalties against Employers & Instructors outlined.

Workshop Conditions – The employer shall provide free of charge, suitable lighting…Heat or fire, if required, between Oct 1st and April 30. Workmen responsible for lighting and feeding the stove or fire. Employer responsible for removal of ashes. Hot water to be provided by employer, free, during recognised meal times. All employers are prohibited from giving subs during the week to any workman.

Goose or Dead Horse – All work to be finished by 12 noon Saturday, before being paid…
All planks to be cleared and left tidy at pay time. Every workman must clean and sweep his own plank out at least once a week… Every employer shall whitewash each workroom at least once per year.

All brown willows to be boiled or soaked by the employer.

List of the Sizes of Baskets, Hampers, Carriages and Perambulators, etc. The Journeymen's Prices affixed for the town of Nottingham, 1872

Extracts from the publication, printed by George Groves of Nottingham

Square Rod Work
- Hose hampers, close
- Meat hampers
- Trimmers' fine, light randed
- Lidded peds
- Bakers' baskets
- Butter maunds
- Skeleton bottle baskets
- Hawkers' baskets
- Slewed starch baskets
- Children's chairs
- Hose hampers, light randed
- Rabbit hampers
- Slewed trimmers
- Packing & upright skips
- Common square baskets
- Lay down bottle baskets
- Counter baskets
- Clothes baskets
- Plumbers' baskets
- Clothes hampers
- Trimmers' close
- Square randed doffs
- Grocers' baskets
- Butter baskets
- Soda & bottle baskets
- Children's panniers
- Show baskets
- Knife baskets

Square Fitched Work
- Box hampers
- Lace baskets
- Fitched fowl baskets
- Roller baskets
- Bobbin baskets
- Bird baskets
- Dress baskets
- Bonnet & unlidded baskets
- Egg baskets

Oval Fitched Work
- Picking baskets
- Chaff baskets
- Rabbit baskets

Round Fitched Work
- Doffs & hen copes
- Cradles
- Gardeners' flaskets
- Carriage work (prams etc)
- Washing baskets
- Rag baskets
- Bonnet baskets
- Bird baskets
- Clothes baskets
- Hand hawkers
- Malt skeps,
- Boiling baskets
- Garden chairs
- Egg baskets
- Butchers' baskets
- Dog baskets
- Plate baskets
- Bread baskets
- Scain (Skein) work

Brown Square Work
- Fruit hampers
- Hare hampers
- Carboys
- Wine hampers
- Strawberry baskets
- Iron hampers
- Grape baskets

Round Work
- Jar Cake
- Potato baskets
- Colwick cheese baskets
- Plant baskets
- Stilton cheese baskets
- Glue covers

Oval Brown Work
- Southports
- Timberwork

Miscellaneous
- Flower stands
- Sparrow traps
- Batwells
- Horse collars
- Cudget baskets
- Grass hoops

Notes
Daily work of nine hours per day at four shilling and sixpence (22½p). If 4 miles from home lodgings to be paid. That every man shall be paid so that he may be clear off the ground by 2 o'clock on a Saturday.

Original booklet in the Newark Museum Collection (ref D.1166)

Thomas Miller of Gainsborough, basket maker and author

Born 31st August, 1807, and lived in St John's Street, Gainsborough. His father was a wharfinger but left the family home for London, leaving behind his wife and children. Thomas had various labouring jobs before being apprenticed to his stepfather. He moved to Retford around 1829, and eventually set up in business on his own as a basket maker. Working a 12 hour day, he made reticules (hair baskets) in three sizes, for 11 shillings per dozen. This fine basketry involved splitting the osiers, known as skein work.

Within 18 months he had moved to Nottingham, in the employment of Mr. Watts, Basket maker at Bromley House. His workshop was in Swan's Yard, Long Row. As he sold his wares on his basketry market stall, he would read out his poetry to potential customers. Such as "Thus while I sung my sorrows I deceived, And bending osiers into baskets weaved…"

Thomas's first book, was published in 1832, and he went on to publish about sixty more. 'Gideon Giles, the Roper', being perhaps his most popular novel. He also composed:

"These osiers by murmuring river grew
That leaned and laughed in sunshine all day
The winds, thin lipped, with their green leaves did play
And on their silvery palms the pearly dew
Hung like the watching stars in night's deep blue
And birds sailed o'er them as the day grew grey
And white waves kissed their stems, then rolled away."

An extract from 'Country Life', 1847… "A beautiful sight, on a spring evening, is that boat returning homeward, laden with osiers, piled so high, that the steersman cannot see the head of the little barque, but is compelled to take his instructions from the man seated on the top of the snow white bunches. The Osier peelers are stowed, thick as bees, in the head and stern of the boat; and the screams of the women, when danger is far distant, form merriment to the passing boatmen".

In 1835 Thomas moved to Southwark, London, and from 1842 - 45 was generally unsuccessful at becoming a publisher of his own works. Shortly before his death, in a state of poor health and wealth, he was granted a £100 pension grant by Disraeli. He died on the 25th October, 1874, and is buried in Norwood Cemetery, London. At Nottingham Castle there is a memorial plaque to Thomas Miller – basket maker and author.

Sources of reference:-
'Thomas Miller' by Cedric Bonnell and reprinted from the Nottinghamshire Express, 1904.
'Thomas Miller' by J.S. English, Gainsborough Library, 1970. and 'T. Miller' by George Morley, 1962.
Gainsborough Library, Local Studies, has a fine collection of books by their famous son.

Lincolnshire basket making families - Wood and Elmore.

The Lincolnshire Elmore and Wood families have a long basket making tradition, and in the case of Elmore, established the largest basket making base in Leicester and a national willow authority.

Elmore

William Elmore arrived in Sleaford in 1767 as a basket maker, said to be from Stamford. Between 1771 – 1781, 5 children were born, William (2)1771, and Richard in 1775 both to become basket makers. William (2) married Mary Palgrave of Sleaford (a surname used as a Christian name for many future Elmores) and in 1793 moved to Horncastle, and had 7 children, of these James born 1794, William (3) born 1796 who married Mary Jackson of Tattershall and had 8 or 9 children. Three of William (3) children were basket makers – Jackson Hall Elmore, William Tayton E, and William Talin and all three were to move to Leicester and establish Leicester's largest basket making firm. The 1881 Census reveals - Jackson Hall Elmore employed 46 workers - 3rd largest in UK, with Harrison of Grantham being the largest.

Jackson Hall's son, William Palgrave, became one of the UK's leading authorities on willow growing, writing a Ministry of Agriculture publication in 1913, and responsible for introducing several French basketry willows into this country. William Palgrave's son, Ernest, a change from William, then continued the business until after World War 2. So the Elmores, or Ellmores, produced 11 basket makers over 6 generations, the first four generations in Lincolnshire and the remainder in Leicestershire.

Wood

The Wood family originated from Norwell, Nottinghamshire, and by 1826 according to White's Trade Directory were in business in Westgate, Grantham. His wife Mary came from Barrowby, and of their children William, Charles and Stephen listed in the 1841 Census all became basket makers.

In the 1861 Census, William was 75 years old, and still a basket maker, his son Stephen was a Master Basket maker on Wharf Road, with his wife and sons - William 7 years, and Frederick 4. William Junior had moved to Newark as a basket maker in Balderton Gate, with his Newark born wife Jane and children including Alfred (15) an apprentice basket maker. From the birth place of the children William must have been in Newark at least since 1846.

By the 1871 Census, Stephen was in Westgate and his son William at 17 years, not surprisingly was a basket maker. Ten years later, Stephen had died and his widow Ann ran the business with sons Arthur Leighton, just 15 years old, and Frederick.

The 1901 Census records nearly all the surviving family had left basket making, only Frederick and William remained, who were grand children of William and Mary, and in turn had produced 10 descendants who were basket makers in Grantham and Newark.

Harrison's of Grantham

Harrison's catalogues state the firm was established in 1710, but the earliest Directory reference located is 1835 when Samuel Harrison is recorded as a basket maker in Walkergate. The 1851 Census, records him as a Master Basket maker (employer). In 1861 he employed 2 men and 2 boys, rising to 3 men and 3 boys with shops in Bourne and Sleaford by 1871, William Brewster having taken over following Samuel's death in 1867.

It was the next Census in 1881, that shows William B's rise to one of the country's leading manufacturers with 73 workers – 40 men, 14 boys and 19 women (plus up to 100 seasonal workers). William B was 42 years old, with his Sleaford born wife Sarah, 40, and six children, all born in Grantham. In the 1905 Kelly's Directory W.B. Harrison & Son is listed as a wholesale and export manufacturers of willow, cane and rush art furniture and willow merchant.

Their large and impressive premises on Watergate was built in 1883, with further extensions in 1889 on the adjoining Union Street site. The Watergate buildings being demolished by 1967 for a supermarket car park.

William Brewster Harrison was prominent in local affairs, elected to Grantham Town Council in 1886 and served as Mayor 1894-5. A fine illuminated address was presented to him to mark the occasion and signed by 156 employees; it now forms part of a display in Grantham Museum. The Library has a number of catalogues and photos relating to the firm in the Local Studies Collection.

Harrison's had Osier beds in Grantham between Dysart Road and Barrowby Road, along the Canal near the Harlaxton Road Swing Bridge and at Dry Doddington and Normanton, with a Buffing and Processing Yard situated on Westbourne Place, off Dysart Road. Harrison is one of a handful of local growers to have a basketry willow named after him Salix harrisoniana, and listed by the Basford grower, William Scaling in 1871.

Following the death of William B in 1908, his son Oliver took over, followed by his two sons, Aubrey and Sidney. The firm became a 'Ltd Co' in 1911. Harrison's also had a perambulator factory in Archer Street, Nottingham, and traded under the name 'Belvoir'. In the 1930s they retailed 'prams' at £30 each – a small fortune. During the 1940s they employed 25 pram workers, working from 8am to 6pm, producing 50 prams per week.

The depression of the 1920s and large scale imports of foreign basketry led to difficult times and following the death of Aubrey and Sidney the Grantham firm closed c.1965, bringing to an end Lincolnshire's largest basketry business.

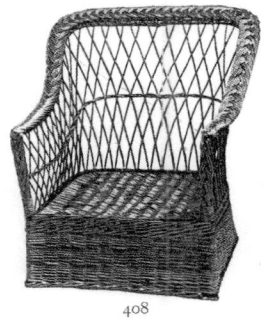

408
Seat 22 x 21in., 11/3.   Seat 25 x 22in., 12/9
Seat 28 x 23in., 15/9

786
Seat 25 x 23in., 14/3.
Best Quality, Seat 25 x 23in., 15/9

788
Seat 20 x 20in., 12/6.   Seat 24 x 22in., 14/9
Seat 26 x 22in., 16/3

A Basketful 31

ILLUSTRATED CATALOGUE
& PRICE LIST
OF GOODS MANUFACTURED BY

WILLIAM HARRISON

WHOLESALE MANUFACTURER

OF

WICKER CHAIRS, SOFAS, TABLES, AND BASKETS,

WILLOW GROWER AND EXPORTER,

17 & 18 WATERGATE,

GRANTHAM.

Steam Buffing Works—Earle's Fields.

Harrison's of Grantham

Made from Best Hard English Willows.

3668
Buff and Green Rush, 16/6

3667
Buff and Green Rush, 11/9

1910
Green Rush, 11/3.   Cream Rush, 13/6

3666
Green Rush and Cream, 12/9.   Cream only 14/9

They are made by SKILLED WORKMEN who have spent a lifetime at the trade.

Page from Harrison's 'Artistic Willow' Catalogue 1912

NETT LIST OF PRICES FOR PERAMBULATORS,—1871.

WILLIAM HARRISON,

MANUFACTURER OF

PERAMBULATORS & BASKETS,

18, WATERGATE, GRANTHAM.

WOOD PERAMBULATORS.

No.	For One Child.	s.	d.	No.	For Two Children.	s.	d.
1.—14 inch Iron Rimmed Wheels		12	0	1.—14 inch Iron Rimmed Wheels		15	0
2.—14 inch Felloed Wheels		15	0	2.—14 inch Felloed Wheels		18	0
3.—16 inch ditto		18	0	3.—16 inch ditto		21	0
4.—18 inch ditto Shakel Springs		22	0	4.—18 inch ditto Shakel Springs		25	0

WICKER PERAMBULATORS.—BUFF.

No.	For One Child.	s.	d.	No.	For Two Children.	s.	d.
1.—Iron Rimmed Wheels		4	0	1.—Side by Side		7	0
2.— ditto		4	6	2.—Face to Face		8	0
3.— ditto		5	0				

Upholstered with American Leather 3/- each extra.   Upholstered with American Leather 4/6 each extra.

The Perambulators in Wood are got up in a good style, well painted, and striped, Upholstered in American Leather Cloth, fitted complete with lapelled waterproof aprons, box capped, strong and well made.

Perambulators lined with Crimson, Green, and Blue Utrecht Velvet, and Broad Cloth— Single, 6/- extra. Double, 8/- extra.

Hoods, single, 5/-   Hoods, double, 7/0.

If fitted with Side Springs, 5/- Best quality, 7/6.

Parashute Holders, in brass, 3/6.

Wicker Inyalid Carriages, Croquet Chairs, Linen Baskets, Clothes Baskets, Nursery Chairs, Wicker Table Mats, Linen Hampers, Travelling Baskets, Reticules, &c., &c.

Harrison's of Grantham

WICKER INVALID CHAIRS.

No. 505

Mounted on bow springs, with fast front.

A. 14in. seat, with 25in. and 12in. ⅝ wired-on tyred wheels

72/-

B. 16in. seat, with 25in. and 12in. ⅝ wired-on tyred wheels

82/-

C. 18in. seat, with 26in. and 12in. ¾ wired-on tyred wheels

96/-

No. 506

Mounted on shackle springs, with guide front.

A. 14in. seat, with 25in. and 12in. ⅝ wired-on tyred wheels, **92/-**

B. 16in. seat, with 25in. and 12in. ⅝ wired-on tyred wheels, **110/-**

C. 18in. seat, with 26in. and 12in. ¾ wired-on tyred wheels, **126/-**

Page from Harrison's 1911 Catalogue of Perambulators, Bassinettes and Mail Carts.

A Basketful 35

Harrison's of Grantham

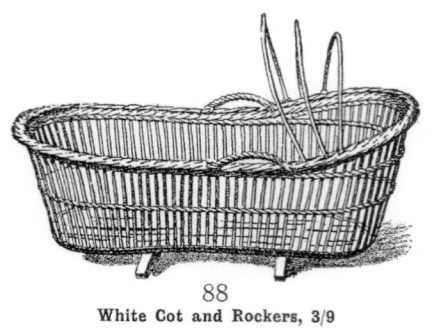

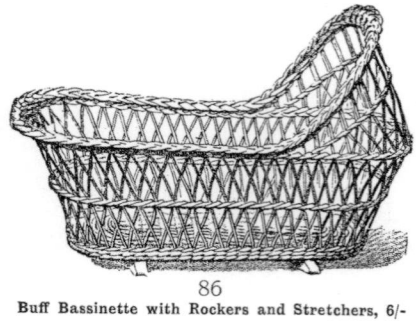

88
White Cot and Rockers, 3/9

86
Buff Bassinette with Rockers and Stretchers, 6/-

Cot and Bassinette from the
'Artistic Willow' catalogue c.1912

William Brewster Harrison,
Mayor of Grantham 1894-5

Harrison Exhibition stand at an unknown location. Must be pre 1911, the year Harrison became 'Co Ltd'
Photos: Mayor and exhibition stand courtesy of Grantham Library.

36   A Basketful

Last of their line – Cyril Wakefield and Charlie Leggitt

Cyril was born in Boston in 1925. When he was 17 he started a 4 year apprenticeship to train as a basket maker at the Royal Midland Association for the Blind on Chaucer Street Nottingham. On completion of his apprenticeship in 1946, Cyril moved back to Boston and set up in business making a wide range of basketry, but concentrating on agricultural baskets to meet local needs. One year he completed an order for 2,000 potato mollies. He also made shopping, angling and laundry baskets and cradles. One of Cyril's cradles made in 1959 is a family heirloom, having already being used for 11 family babes.

Most of Cyril's willows came from Somerset and buying in quantity with fellow local blind basket makers Mr. Hancock and Richard Hogg, who were also trained at Nottingham. One of Cyril's most interesting projects was to make a replica medieval screen for Gainsborough Old Hall. He was also a regular and popular demonstrator at Church Farm Museum at Skegness. Cyril retired in 1997, following a stroke, and his tools were presented to the Museum of Lincolnshire Life.

I first met Charlie Leggitt in 1971 in his overgrown willow holt next to his Saxilby home. Charlie was not in the best of health and a youngish, enthusiastic researcher, was just what he needed. With expert tuition from Charlie, the author and several pressed friends and colleagues harvested Charlie's willows. Several tons, about 100,000 overgrown rods, and growers were right "Osier cutting is the hardest work – stooping from morning until night..." Charlie found a smile, and put it down to experience!

A few weeks later he had made me an eel hive to a local pattern plus a sieve with a fine skein centre. Charlie's willows, mainly Black Maul and Wissenders, provided sets for several other locations and the film back drop for a "rustic scene" in a television drama, and my hands were shown stripping the willow. The following year, as a result of the willow holt experience, an educational filmstrip was made by professional film maker Paul Graham and distributed nationally, but unfortunately it was pre-video and CD/DVD era.

Cyril Wakefield. Photo taken 2006

Charlie Leggitt with his willow bolts, c.1972

Mills of Southwell and Newark

John Horace Mills was born in 1856, the eldest son of John Mills of East Leake where the Mills family were major basket makers in the village. When John Horace wished to set up in business in 1882, he felt the need to establish himself in Southwell, his late mother's home town. He started a willow growing and basket making firm on Kirklington Road, but had difficulty in recruiting his work force. As his 15 year lease drew to a close, John Horace looked to Newark, and moved there in 1897.

The Newark factory premises were a former seed crushing mill beside the River Trent and offered space and opportunity. The local newspaper, the Newark Advertiser, records in 1896 Mills had 50 workers in Southwell, turning out 280 chairs per week. Upholstering of wicker chairs also started that year. Mills had 80 acres for cultivating the willows in Southwell alone, employing 39 seasonal rod peelers and buffing 400 tons of willow in that year. Willow stripping was done at Farndon crossroads, Victoria Gardens Newark and Balderton. (See the 1918 advert on page 21 for 20 women wanted).

By 1899 his willow acreage increased and included Southwell, Fiskerton, Morton, Farndon, Claypole and Dry Doddington. Basketry production rose to 300 chairs per week and during the year delivered over 1,000 potato and pea baskets to Nottingham. Transport was by horse and cart, six hours each way, with eleven horses stabled at Newark. The workforce was around 100, 65 at Newark and the remainder at Southwell. The chief line of business was wicker furniture – chairs, tables, whatnots, settees and upholstered goods, which were sent as far afield as Aberdeen and Eastbourne.

John Horace Mills stated "the finest quality rods grown in this country are those from Nottinghamshire. You have only to guarantee the osier to be grown in Nottinghamshire to be able to sell them readily anywhere". He went on to say "he had just bought a further 14 acres at Fiskerton, for turning into a willow holt". Wages were quoted at girls and women and learners 8 shillings (40p) per week, lads 6,7 or 8 shillings depending on proficiency. The Southwell wage bill was £40 weekly.

John Horace said the Mills family had five basket making generations, starting with his grandfather's grandfather at West Leake. Mark Mills, a relation employed 50 at East Leake and another cousin Nathan also had a workshop there – the staple industry of East Leake.

In 1913 Mills was making side cars for motor cycles and claimed to be the largest manufacturer in Britain. Two years later he also claimed to be the largest willow grower in the country. He increased the use of cane for furniture production, trading as 'orrisMils' and later 'Sunreed' and 'Trent Loom' by 1957. John Horace died in 1941 and had three sons in the business, Horace Arthur, William Edward and John Harold (my informant) who died in 1978. The factory having closed c.1964. A recent housing development adjoining the factory has been appropriately named 'The Osiers', a reminder of this once important local industry.

Horace Mills of Newark

Mills factory (a former seed crushing mill) on Farndon Road, Newark, c.1980.

View of the chair frame workshop, Newark, c.1928, producing up to 300 chairs per week.

Weaving the chair seats and backs on the production line, c.1926.

Four chair workers, c.1943 at the Newark factory.

Horace and Marion Mills, with 84 staff and workers, at their Golden Wedding celebration, 1933, outside their home 'Rushcliffe'. Their home was built in 1902, and named after his South Nottinghamshire (East Leake) roots. Photo: Newark Library.

Horace Mills of Newark

A break during War time production of hampers and panniers, 1917. Photo Newark Museum

Letter from America found at the Farndon Road factory site – from Bailie Basket Co., Somerville, Mass. USA to Horace Mills August 1923 …

"It would appear to the present writer that samples of your willows would not be necessary, because he is well acquainted with Nottinghamshire willows, and knows their quality. Therefore, if you are offering us white willows of your own growth, we are willing to take your word for it. Providing we find that the willows will work satisfactorily into chairs, we can assure you that a five or ten ton order will follow shortly".

An international reputation!

Well laden horse and cart with chairs on its way from the factory, c.1930. Driver John Toon of Farndon. Photo via Barry Wheatcroft.

40   A Basketful

The Beestons of Blyth

Four generations of Beestons were basket making in Blyth. The earliest, John Beeston was born in East Stoke. This Trentside village has a number of basket making associations, including the Gee family who were scuttle makers over several generations (William Gee 1740s, Peter his son 1770s and his son Francis - 1841 and 1851 Census).

John Beeston had moved to Blyth by 1842 and his seven children were born there, with sons Richard and William, a basket maker and scuttle maker respectively. Richard also had seven children to continue the basket making tradition into another generation, with John Henry, born c.1875 and Charles E c.1876. Charles' son Frank was then a basket maker until his retirement in the 1970s. I recall visiting Frank at his workshop and his freshly harvested willow holt just outside the village. The memory has faded less however, than the slide I took to record the visit, fortunately the Bassetlaw Museum at Retford have the two photographs shown here.

Photo right from the Edgar Welchman Collection. shows Frank at his plank, c.1970.

Workshop signboard in the Retford Museum Collection

A Basketful

Rawsons of Elston

The photograph is of John W. Rawson, a specialist skep maker. Skeps are heavy duty containers for bulky materials and used locally for gypsum at the plaster pits, for coal deliveries (before hessian/jute sacks) and as malt containers. Making skeps was hard work, involving splitting or riving ash for a frame with the remainder woven in willow. John had a reputation for quality skeps, often working in bare feet, leaving both hands for weaving the rods. Once, around 1914, for a wager, he made a skep that held water, no mean feat, made out of willow. John was the last of five Rawsons, through three generations.

The family originated from Barton in Fabis, near Nottingham. In Barton in 1841 and 1851 a George Rawson was a basket maker and his son George also, but sadly died just 26 years old.

The Elston branch through John, born at Barton c.1788 had moved to East Stoke/Elston by the 1830s, married Ann from Tickhill, and had two sons George b 1836 and John b c.1845, both basket and scuttle makers. George in turn had nine children two of them being basket makers – Henry born c.1866 and John born 1868. By 1901, Henry had left basket making for gardening, but John continued the craft beyond his retirement into the 1950s.

The Rawsons had willow holts in Elston between the village and nearby Sibthorpe and also Cotham Lane, near the River Devon. Many villagers welcomed the seasonal work of peeling Rawson's rods, including the author's grandmother.

42   A Basketful

Emile Janssens of Newark

Emile Janssens' exhibition stand at the British Industries Fair, possibly at Olympia, c.1947

Born around 1890, Emile came to England as a Belgian refugee c.1915, and was a basket maker in Belgium. With the support of Marshall's of Sutton on Trent, he took a shop in Newark, firstly North Gate then Middle Gate, with a compatriot Remoortere, and up to 1940 had his workshop in Chatham Street. At an Industries Fair, Queen Mary bought one of his baskets and at the sides of the above Exhibition stand, a card proudly proclaims his Royal patronage. In 1943, his workshop moved to Portland Street until his death c.1952. At his peak, he employed up to 40 workers, and specialised in decorative shopping baskets. This lovely photograph comes via a talk from one of his daughters.

Harry Summers of Sutton on Trent

Harry was the third generation of his family – basket makers. His father and grand father were both basket makers and named Thomas, Harry's father Thomas b.1872, his brother Joseph b.1875 and sister Lizzie b.1870, all born at Sutton, and all became basket makers. Their father Thomas b.1845 and his brother Henry b.1848 in Newark, were listed as apprentice basket makers in Newark (1861 Census).

Thomas Senior's father, (Harry's great grandfather) John was a shoe maker in Newark. Thomas and Henry moved to Sutton on Trent c.1868, following the boom after the buffing discovery. Henry later moved as a basket maker to Scotland (1881 Census). Thomas became Master Basket Maker until 1925, when his son Thomas took over. Harry succeeded him in 1948 until his death in 1977 – (interview with Harry 1973). Four of Harry's brothers did not follow their father's occupation and emigrated to Canada.

I visited and interviewed Harry many times, took photos - b/w and slide, helped produce an educational film strip with professional photographer Paul Graham, and observed angling and potato baskets being made from start to finish.

Harry was the last full time basket maker in Nottinghamshire, and led me to realise the importance and urgency to record this area's valuable contribution to basketry and employment. Although much was seasonal, it was locally an important source of income.

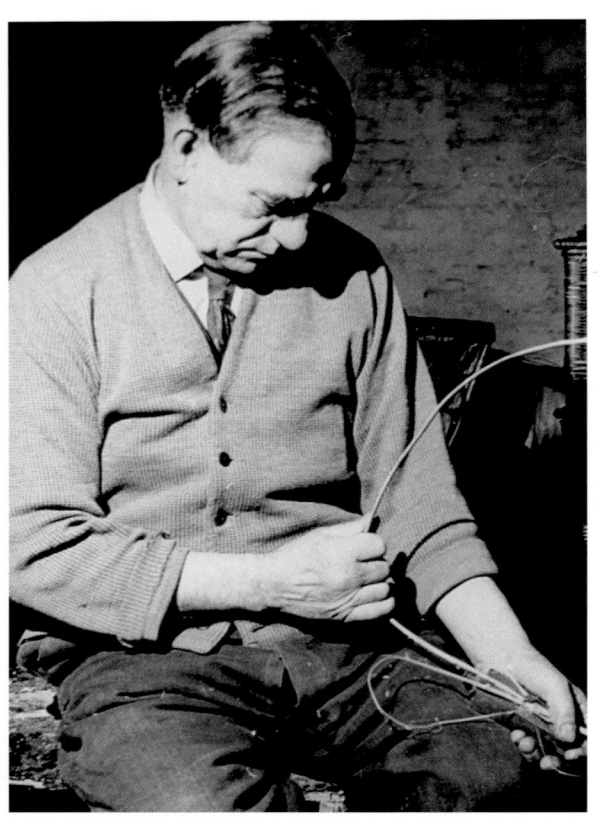

Harry Summers and Frank Bennett, 1960

Harry using a shave for skein work, 1971.
Photo: Pauline Heathcote L.R.P.S.

The shop situated in front of the workshop, High Street, Sutton on Trent.
Photo: picturethepast, Reg Baker, 1984.

Basket making migration to Sutton on Trent

The Taylors of Sutton on Trent c.1900. One of several basket making families that came to the village following the 'buffing' discovery c.1868. Photo shows second from right, William James Taylor and far right, thought to be his father William, who was recorded as a basket maker at Sutton in the 1871 Census and born in Mawdesley, Lancashire. Also from the 1871 Census and Mawdesley, came Peter Marsden, William Welch and William Heys, who had a 2 year old son born in Sutton on Trent, proving the migration took place by 1869. Photo: via Terry Fry of Basford.

John Olko came over as a Polish airman and stayed with Marshall's and Harry Summers. He made baskets up to c.1980, when this photo was taken. Photo via Mrs P. Butt.

The Roulstones and Albert Newton

The remarkable Roulstones; between 1851 and the 1901 Census 24 different members of the Roulstone family were in basket making. The family roots were in Radcliffe on Trent, then spread to other, and perhaps more sought after, areas such as East Leake and Castle Donington in Leicestershire.

William (the elder) was born in Radcliffe on Trent around 1774, and was listed in the 1851 Census as a 77 year old basket maker, with seven other Roulstones recorded in the village as basket makers. No wonder two had moved out by the 1861 Census, to Radford and Sherwood which were expanding suburbs of Nottingham. By 1871, they were in East Leake and in 1881 Castle Donington, just over the border.

Few Roulstones established firms of their own, although without doubt they had the skills, but perhaps not the financial resources. Of the 24 known Roulstone basket makers, 18 were born in Radcliffe on Trent, four in Castle Donington and two in East Leake, but all no doubt regarded Radcliffe as their ancestral home.

By 1932 Frederick and Alexander Roulstone were listed as joint owners of the Central Basket Works (formerly Matthew Mills), but by this date willow basket making was in serious decline, mainly through cheap imports and alternative materials for containers. Roulstones had woven the last of their magic.

A lovely photograph taken about 1938 of Albert Newton, hamper maker of Park Lane, Basford.

46   A Basketful

Basford, Nottingham

Around 1900, Basford had the largest concentration of wicker furniture and perambulator manufacturers in the UK, with several factories each employing over 300 workers.

Alexandra Works, built in 1901, on the corner of Egypt Road and Radford Road. The factory of Danish born Peter Mathieson. Photo taken 2001.

The Springfield Works, 2001 Morris, Wilkinson's factory, Radford Road / Chelmsford Road

Goad's Insurance map, c.1910 identifies the 'risk factors' with each of the three factories.

Another factory site of Morris, Wilkinson, known as the Victoria Works, and built in 1896 with offices above the archway and upholstery workshops on right. Photo 2001.

A Basketful 47

SPRINGFIELD BASKET & PERAMBULATOR WORKS.

THOMAS CHAMBERS,
BASKET MANUFACTURER, WILLOW IMPORTER, & GENERAL DEALER
BASFORD, NOTTINGHAM.

HOSE HAMPERS	BRUSHES
LACE DITTO	MATS
BLEACHERS' DITTO	HARDWARE
TRAVELLING DITTO	COOPERY WARE
WICKER PARCEL CONVEYANCES	CLOTHES LINES
INVALID CARRIAGES	WASH LEATHERS
BASSINETTES	FANCY SOAPS
PERAMBULATORS	SPONGES
WICKER CHAIRS, TABLES,	FLOOR FLANNELS
And every description of Basket Work made to order.	And a great variety of Useful and Ornamental Articles.

AGENT FOR THE
PATENT COMBINED PERAMBUCOT & CRADLE.

By one motion of the lever, which extends the rockers at the same time, the cradle is released from the wheels, and is ready for use. By this simple arrangement, should the child be asleep on reaching home, or when out visiting, it is needless to waken it, the cradle can be released, carried into the room, and the child left undisturbed.

Price List of the Patent Combined Perambucot (Bassinette) and Cradle.

No. 1—Fitted on 24in. Spider Wheels with India Rubber Tyres, upholstered in "Crockett's" American Leather, genuine Steel Springs, Buff Wicker Body, Hood and China Handle, Brass Hood Joints, Springs and Wheels artistically lined ... £4 8 0

No. 2—Same as No. 1, upholstered in Carriage Cloth ... £4 11 0

No. 3—Black Japanned Wicker Body, upholstered, &c., same as No. 1 ... £4 11 0

No. 4—Black Japanned Wicker Body, upholstered in Carriage Cloth, same as No. 2 ... £4 12 0

The Upholstering may be had in any Colour to order.

ORDINARY PERAMBUCOTS.

	£	s.	d.
A.—"The Durable," fitted on 24in. Spider Wheels, India Rubber Tyres, upholstered in "Crockett's" American Leather, Genuine Steel Springs, Buff Wicker Body, Hood and China Handle, Brass Hood Joints, Springs and Wheels artistically lined	3	15	6
B.—"The Durable," same as A, upholstered in Carriage Cloth	3	18	6
C.—"The Durable" Black, Japanned Wicker Body, fitted same a A	3	18	6
D.—"The Durable," Black Japanned Body, fitted same as B	4	1	0

WILLIAM PERKINS,
MANUFACTURER OF
SOUTHPORT BASKETS, PERAMBULATORS,
AND BUFF-ROD WORK IN GENERAL,
CARRINGTON WORKS, CARRINGTON,
NOTTINGHAM.

JOHN KINGSTON,
BASKET AND PERAMBULATOR MAKER,

MANUFACTURER OF

WICKER PERAMBULATORS,

WICKER INVALID CARRIAGES,

TOY PERAMBULATORS,

AND

BASKET WORK OF EVERY DESCRIPTION

Including all kinds of

JAPANNED WICKER WORK.

ORDERS PROMPTLY ATTENDED TO.   NOTE THE ADDRESS:

QUEEN ST. BASKET WORKS, OLD BASFORD, NOTTINGHAM.

C. ROYSTON,
WILLOW MERCHANT,

ALBERT STREET AND PARK WHARF,

NOTTINGHAM.

MANUFACTURER OF

HAMPERS, SKEPS, LACE BASKETS, &C.

PORTMANTEAUS, TRUNKS, TRAVELLING BAGS, BRUSHES, COCOA MATS & MATTING.

C. ANGERSBACH,

MANUFACTURER OF ALL KINDS OF

BERLIN BASKETS

And Willow Furniture,

HIGH STREET, OLD BASFORD,

NEAR NOTTINGHAM

East Leake – a village with a rich basket making tradition

A delightful photograph, showing a nest of three lunch baskets and a Croquet Chair, made by Frank Bramley, c.1910.

East Leake – the Bramleys

Frank Bramley with willow and rush chairs c.1910. Three brothers, Joseph, Frank and George Henry; Joseph the willow grower and the other two basket makers. The author met Frank's son Robert, who did not follow basket making, but kindly loaned the photographs for copying in 1972, which are now in the Local Studies Library Collection, Nottingham. Below is another example of Frank's skills, a cycle trailer he designed c.1910. Rider and cyclist sat back to back.

A Basketful

East Leake – the Mills dynasty

Shell Workers at Matthew Mills factory at East Leake c.1915. Note the lapel badges many are wearing, which featured a shell and showed they were on essential War work.
Photo: picturethepast

Catalogue cover c.1950 of Mark W Mills 'Beehive Works'. Note 'established over 200 years'.
The firm can be traced back to Robert Mills in the 18th century, Mark William was his great grandson and Christopher being Mark William's great grandson. That's a great family history, tradition and a basket making dynasty few could rival.

Lincolnshire basket makers 1790 – 1850, sourced from Trade Directories.

Name	Location	Address	1790	1822	1826	1835	1842	1849
Arch Joseph	Deeping St James					0		
Ashton John	Louth	East Gate			0			
Bagnall Phillip	Donington				0			
Barratt George	Lincoln	Waterside			0	0	0	0
Barrick William	Barrow on Humber						0	0
Baxter John	Lincoln	Eastgate	0					
Bennett Charles	Gainsborough	Caskgate		0				
Bishop James	Horncastle	Far St					0	
Bostock William	Long Sutton					0		
Boswell Edward	Louth	Eastgate					0	0
Bull Isaac	Stamford	Broad Street				0		0
Camomile Joseph	Sleaford	Southgate			0	0	0	0
Camomile Joseph	Lincoln	High Street				0		
Carter William	Gainsborough	Beastmarket				0		
Chapman Richard	Lincoln	Brayford Street					0	0
Chapman William	Lincoln	Waterside				0	0	0
Colton Catherine	Brigg						0	
Corley Thomas	Spalding	Herring Lane					0	
Crampton Wm Thos	Boston	High Street						0
Crane Robert	Epworth	Market Place				0	0	
Curtis Jane	Lincoln	Waterside				0		
Curtis Samuel	Lincoln	Waterside				0		
Curtois John	Lincoln	Waterside	0					
Curtois William	Lincoln	High Street	0					
Dales Charles Jnr	Alford	South End				0		
Dallicoat George	Spalding	Sheep Market/Hall St				0	0	0
Dallicoat Robert	Spalding	Reform Street				0		0
Dawson William	Louth	Eastgate			0	0	0	
Deveroux Miller	Louth	Vicar Lane				0		
Dobson George	Boston	Church Street					0	
Dowse Edward	Louth	Eastgate			0	0	0	0
Dowse William	Louth	Bridge Street						0
Duncan Thomas	Gainsborough	Caskgate			0	0	0	0
Ellmore Jackson Hall	Sleaford	Southgate						0
Ellmore William	Boston	High Sreet				0		
Ellmore William	Horncastle	Far Street				0		
Ellmore William P	Sleaford	Southgate				0	0	0
Ellmore Charles	Horncastle	Far Street				0		
Etches James	Brigg	Black Bull Yd/Scawby St				0	0	
Fields George	Horncastle	Far Street					0	
Fisher William	Lincoln	St Mary's St					0	
Freeman Isaac	Long Sutton				0			

Lincolnshire basket makers 1790 – 1850, sourced from Trade Directories.

Name	Location	Address	1790	1822	1826	1835	1842	1849
Gee William	Lincoln	High St					0	
Glew John	Grantham	Walkergate			0	0		
Glew William	Grantham	Westgate					0	
Glew William	Boston / Stamford			0	0	0		
Graves Frederick	Horncastle	Market Place					0	
Green Robert	Louth	Spital Lane				0		
Greenwood D	Stamford	Red Lion St						0
Harrison Samuel	Grantham	Watergate					0	0
Howitt W	Crowland	Church St						0
Ingoldby James	Louth					0		
Jarvis John	Louth	Walkergate				0		
Jarvis Joseph	Louth	Eastgate					0	
Jee John & Son	Spilsby						0	
Jee Joseph	Alford						0	
Jee Sarah & Sons	Spilsby / Alford						0	0
Johnson Thomas	Gainsborough	Market Place					0	0
Lansdale Hamerton	Spalding	Double Street					0	0
Leighton Lewis	Lincoln	Waterside				0		
Linwood John	Gainsborough	Casket Lane				0		
Low Benjamin	Spilsby					0		
Lyon Charles	Stamford	Peter's Hill					0	
Lyon W	Stamford	Broad St						0
Markillie Jacob	Long Sutton						0	
Mason William	Spalding	New Road					0	0
May S	Owston Ferry							0
Mitchell Thomas	Grimsby	Deansgate						0
Molson John	Swineshead	Hamond Back Bridge				0		
Moor Samuel	Swineshead					0		
Moore Leonard	Swineshead						0	0
Morris Edward	Market Rasen	Bridge Street		0	0	0		
Moulson John	Boston	West Street				0		
Nicholson Richard	Horncastle	Buttermarket				0	0	
Norris Edward	Boston	Bridge Street					0	0
Norris John	Boston	High Street		0	0	0		
Owen Richard	Lincoln	High Street				0	0	0
Patrick Samuel	Lincoln	High Street					0	0
Phillips Joseph	Boston	Fountain Lane					0	0
Pocklington Peter	Long Sutton					0		
Pocklington William	L Sutton / Holbeach			0	0		0	
Purkis John	Crowle					0		
Ratcliffe George	Stamford	Red Lion Square				0	0	0
Reddey Thomas	Sleaford	Eastgate					0	

54   A Basketful

Lincolnshire basket makers 1790 – 1850, sourced from Trade Directories.

Name	Location	Address	1790	1822	1826	1835	1842	1849
Reed Thomas	Alford	South End				0		
Rhodes Ann	Louth	Watergate		0				
Rhodes John	Spalding	Bridge Street				0		
Rhodes Joshua	Spalding	New Road			0			
Robinson John	Boston	High Street		0	0	0	0	
Robinson Thos	Grantham	Walkergate					0	
Ruff William	Spilsby					0		
Saxby Richard	Gainsborough	Bridge Street		0				
Smith Ann	Sleaford	Eastgate				0		
Smith Henry	Horncastle	St Lawrence St					0	
Snart Henry	Lincoln / Meth'ham					0	0	0
Spencer B H	Deeping St James					0		
Spicer Matthew	Gainsborough	Market Place						0
Stubbins Mary	Brigg	Bridge Street				0	0	0
Tabor Geo Young	Deeping St Jas						0	0
Tabor Thomas	Bourne			0	0	0		
Tabor Thomas	Market Deeping					0	0	0
Taylor William	Gainsborough	Bridge Street				0	0	0
Templeman John	Deeping St Jas						0	0
Walker William	Gainsborough	Church St					0	
Waltham William	Spalding / Bourne						0	0
Ward William	Bourne	North Street					0	0
Watkinson John & Son	Gainsborough	Beastmarket					0	
Webb John	Gainsborough	Casket Lane				0		
Wells Joseph	Louth	Eastgate					0	0
Whelpton John	Gainsborough	Church Lane				0		
White J	Holbeach							0
White Samuel	Holbeach					0		
Winter William	Boston	High Street					0	0
Wood William	Grantham	Westgate				0	0	0
Woodcock Thomas	Spilsby						0	
Wright Charles	Lincoln	High Street						0
Younger J	Spilsby							0

Chair illustrations from W.B. Harrison's of Grantham 'Artistic Willow' catalogue 1912

Lincolnshire basket makers - 1850 - 1900

(Sourced from Census 1861 and 1881 and Trade directories from 1872 and 1889).

Name	Address	Birthplace	Birth	BM Detail	1861	1872	1881	1889
Adkinson Henry	Grantham, Westgate	Grantham	1862	BM			0	
Aistrup Thomas	Spalding, London Rd	Bourne	1854	BM			0	0
Altoft George	Barton St Mary	Bonby	1857	BM (blind)			0	0
Anderson Louis	Grimsby, Cavossos Yd	Warw. Birmingham	1833	BM			0	
Ash Richard	Grantham, Spittlegate	Staffs, Willenhall	1861	BM			0	
Ball Thomas	Grantham, Castlegate	Lancs, Southport	1850	BM			0	
Bannister John	Grimsby, Wellowgate	Middx, Hammersmith	1824	BM	0			
Barratt George	Lincoln, Waterside North	Newark	1792	BM	0			
Barratt Henry	Bourne, Church Street	Grantham	1844	BM etc			0	0
Barratt James	Lincoln, Harvey Court	Lincoln	1819	BM			0	
Barratt John	Lincoln, Bells Passage	Lincoln	1801	BM			0	
Barrett Charles	Spalding, Double Street	Lincoln	1806	BM			0	
Barrett Henry	Lincoln, Gaunt Street	Market Rasen	1826	BM	0			
Barrett James	Lincoln, St Marks Place	Lincoln	1819	BM	0		0	
Barrett Robert	Lincoln, St Marks Place	Lincoln	1846	BM	0			
Barrick Ernest	Barrow on Humber	Barrow	1865	BM appr			0	
Barrick James	Barrow on Humber	Barrow	1830	BM		0	0	
Barrick James	Barrow on Humb. Barton Rd	Barrow	1800	BM	0			
Barrick John	Barrow on Humber	Barrow	1796	BM	0	0		
Barrick Samuel	Barrow on Humb. Barton Rd	Barrow	1826	BM	0			
Barrick Thomas	Barrow on Humb. Barton Rd	Barrow	1828	BM	0			
Barrick William	Barrow, St Mary Street	Barrow	1833	BM Empl 5	0		0	0
Bates George	Crowland, Poors Lane	Crowland	1864	BM appr			0	
Bedford William	Horncastle, Market Place	Hants, Earith	1849	BM		0	0	0
Beeden Thomas	Manthorpe	Silk Willoughby	1826	BM			0	
Belton Edward	Horncastle, Millstone St	Horncastle	1831	BM	0			
Belton Francis	Horncastle, Far St	Horncastle	1839	BM	0		0	
Belton James	Horncastle, Far St	Horncastle	1844	BM	0			
Bickerstaffe Mark	Manthorpe, Mission Place	Lancs, Ormskirk	1856	BM			0	
Bingham Richard	Manthorpe, Prospect Place	Northants, Maxey	1831	BM			0	0
Bishop Cornelius	Lincoln, Hungate	Lincoln	1824	BM	0			
Bishop James	Grantham, Walkergate	Horncastle	1816	BM	0			
Bishop William F	Manthorpe, North Street	London	1858	BM			0	
Bodsworth J	Grimsby, Flottergate	Grimsby	1852	BM			0	
Borman King & William	Louth, James Street	Louth		BM			0	
Borrill William	Grimsby, Duke Street	Yorks, Hull	1846	BM			0	
Boswell Benjamin E	Louth, Eastgate	Louth	1864	BM			0	0
Boswell Edward	Louth, Eastgate	Louth	1807	BM	0	0		
Boswell James	Louth, Eastgate	Louth	1832	BM	0	0	0	0
Bradbury Charles	Manthorpe, James Street	Leics, Loughbor.	1846	BM			0	
Brewster William	Grantham, Bradleys Yd	Grantham	1839	BM	0			

Lincolnshire basket makers - 1850 - 1900
(Sourced from Census 1861 and 1881 and Trade directories from 1872 and 1889).

Name	Address	Birthplace	Birth	BM Detail	1861	1872	1881	1889
Briggs Henry	Boston, Petticoat Lane	Boston	1819	BM			0	
Brown Edward	Horncastle, Prospect Place	Essex, Plastow	1859	BM			0	0
Brown Ira	Cleethorpes, High St	Cleethorpes	1867	BM appr			0	
Browning Edward	Grimsby, Nelson Street	Essex, Barking	1865	BM			0	
Bull Isaac	Stamford, then Workhouse	Northants, Islip	1802	BM	0	0	0	
Bull Richard	Stamford, Star Lane	Stamford	1835	BM	0			
Burrows John S & Mrs	Lincoln, St Mary's St			BM	0	0		0
Butcher George	Cleethorpes, Thrunscoe Rd	Laceby	1858	BM			0	
Camomile Joseph	Sleaford, South St	Notts, Brough	1797	BM	0	0		
Chapman John	Horncastle, Foundry St	Lincoln	1810	BM	0			
Chapman Joseph	Horncastle, Far St	Horncastle	1823	BM	0	0	0	
Child Lee	Lincoln, High Street	Lincoln	1838	BM	0		0	
Clarke John T	Thorpe St..Peter	Thorpe St Peter	1842	BM (blind)	0		0	
Cobley Sarah	Grimsby, Kent Street	Yorks, Hull	1844	BM			0	0
Coffee John	Brigg, Change Alley	Horncastle	1851	BM			0	
Colewell Thomas	Horncastle, St Lawrence Ln	Ireland	1835	BM	0			
Commins Emily	Grantham, Wilkins Place	Grantham	1862	BM			0	
Coppin John	Louth, Eastgate	Horncastle	1826	BM Empl	0	0	0	0
Cotton George H	Deeping St James	Keelby	1862	BM			0	
Coultas Charles	Clee, Spencer Street	Essex, Barking	1844	BM			0	
Covill William	Lincoln, High Street	Miningsby	1847	BM appr.	0			
Craddock Charles	Stamford, Scotgate	Stamford	1846	BM appr	0			
Crampton William.	Boston, Wormgate	Boston	181?	BM	0			
Cressey? George	Lincoln, High Street	Broughton	1848	BM appr.	0			
Cross George	Horncastle, Stockshill	Horncastle	1842	BM (blind)	0	0		
Daines Thomas D	Grimsby, Victoria Street	Suffolk, Ixworth	1834	BM			0	
Dallicoat Robert	Spalding, Hall Place			BM		0		
Dobson George J	Grimsby, Fildes Street	Yorks, Leeds	1841	BM			0	
Donner William	Barrow on Humber	Scamblesby	1836	BM			0	0
Dowse William	Louth, Trinity Lane	Louth	1850	BM			0	
Dowse William	Louth, Eastgate	Louth	1819	BM	0	0	0	
Drakes Frederick	Grimsby, Albion Street	Suffolk, Mildenhall	1861	BM			0	
Drakes Saml William	Grimsby, Fish Dock			BM		0		
Drakes Thomas	Grimsby/Washingborough	Suffolk, Mildenhall	1855	BM			0	0
Dring Charles	Burton Coggles	Burton Coggles	1831	BM (blind)			0	0
Duke James	Grimsby, Market Place			BM		0		
Edwards Joseph	Lincoln, High Street	Lincoln	1829	BM	0		0	
Ellis James	Grimsby, Nelson Street	Yorks, Hull	1846	BM			0	
Ellmore James	Sleaford, West Bank	Sleaford	1803	BM	0			
Feltham James	Grimsby, Garden Street	Wilts, Salisbury	1818	BM	0			
Fields William	Gainsborough, Market St	Horncastle	1832	BM	0		0	

Lincolnshire basket makers - 1850 - 1900

(Sourced from Census 1861 and 1881 and Trade directories from 1872 and 1889).

Name	Address	Birthplace	Birth	BM Detail	1861	1872	1881	1889
Fish George	Owston Ferry	Owston Ferry	1853	BM			0	0
Foundation Richard	Grimsby, Upper Burgess St	Notts, Radford	1859	BM			0	
France James	Grimsby, Silver Street	Cleethorpes	1846	BM	0		0	
France Joseph	Grimsby, Worsley St	Cleethorpes	1802	BM			0	
Friend Charles	Stamford, Belton Street	Lancs, Heywood	1861	BM			0	0
Fuller Henry	Grimsby, Osborne St	London	1825	BM	0		0	
Fuller Joseph	Clee, Willingham Street	Grimsby	1866	BM			0	
Gee William	Lincoln, High Street	East Stoke	1817	BM	0	0	0	
Genney W	Grimsby, Flottergate	Grimsby	1850	BM			0	0
Genney William	Grimsby, Market Place	Grimsby	1814	BM Empl	0	0	0	
Glew William	Stamford, Sheepmarket	Boston	1798	BM	0			
Goodacre William	Grantham, Well Lane	Grantham	1863	BM			0	
Graby Robert	Lincoln, Foundry Court	Lincoln	1825	BM	0			
Graves Henry	Grimsby, Freshney Street	Yorks, Selby	1856	BM			0	
Hall Arthur C	Manthorpe, Sydney Street	Worksop	1860	BM			0	
Hall John	Spilsby, Chapel Yard	Toynton	1862	BM			0	
Hall Thomas	Crowland, Poors Lane	Crowland	1843	BM			0	0
Hancock John	Grimsby, Pinfold Hill	Boston	1812	BM	0		0	
Hancock Joseph	Grimsby, Cartergate	Louth	1842	BM	0		0	
Harlock L	Grimsby, Flottergate	Cambridge	1829	BM			0	
Harlock W	Grimsby, Flottergate	Cambridge	1857	BM			0	
Harris Edward	Grimsby, Victoria St West	Devon, Exeter	1821	BM		0	0	
Harris Edward	Grimsby, Albert Street	Norfolk, Yarmouth	1842	BM			0	
Harris Josiah	Clee, Trinity Street	Norfolk, Yarmouth	1850	BM			0	0
Harrison Samuel	Grantham, Watergate	Boston	1816	BM	0			
Harrison Walter	Manthorpe, New Street	Leics, Castle Don.	1844	BM			0	
Harrison Wm Brewster	Bourne / Grantham	Grantham	1839	Manuf		0	0	0
Hartley Joseph	Grimsby, Nelson Street	Yorks, Hull	1855	BM			0	
Hawley Frederick	Grimsby, Eastgate	Grimsby	1860	BM (deaf/dumb)			0	
Hinton A	Grimsby, Freeman St			BM		0		
Hotchen Edwd Overton	Boston, Paddock Grove	Boston	1846	BM			0	
Hubbard William	Bourne, North St	Stamford	1836	BM	0			
Illingworth John	Bourne, North St	Rutland, Oakham	1838	BM appr	0			
J.L.	Lincoln Asylum, B'bridge	Spilsby	1811	BM (former)	0			
Jackson Alfred	Boston, West St	Boston	1817	BM	0			
James John	Gainsborough, Church St	Yorks, Sheffield	1833	BM	0	0	0	
Joules Jonathan W	Grimsby, Holles Street	Yorks, Hull	1843	BM			0	
Kennedy Annie	Manthorpe	Surrey, Rotherhithe	1851	BM			0	
Kennedy Catherine	Grantham, Spittlegate	Ireland	1833	BM			0	
Kennedy William	Grantham, Spittlegate	Lancs, Liverpool	1855	BM			0	
Kidd William	Boston, Mill Lane	Louth	1850	BM			0	

Lincolnshire basket makers - 1850 - 1900
(Sourced from Census 1861 and 1881 and Trade directories from 1872 and 1889).

Name	Address	Birthplace	Birth	BM Detail	1861	1872	1881	1889
King John & William	Manthorpe	Grantham	1862	BM			0	
Kirk Joseph	Lincoln, Gray Street	Scopwick	1845	BM (blind)			0	0
Knight William	Louth, Aswell Lane	Kelstern	1856	BM (blind)			0	0
Lansdall Hamerton	Spalding, Double St	Horncastle	1810	BM	0	0	0	
Latter Harry	Grantham, Spittlegate	Great Gonerby	1857	BM			0	0
Longborough Thomas	Grimsby, Wellowgate	Yorks, Hull	1836	BM	0			
Louth William	Stamford, All Saint's St			BM		0		
Loveday C	Stamford, St Leonard's St			BM		0		
Ludaman? Wm	Gainsborough	Germany?	1836	BM	0			
Lyon Mary	Stamford, Broad Street	Stamford	1825	Bsket Shopkpr.			0	0
Lyon William	Stamford, Broad Street	Rutland, Ketton	1833	BM	0	0		
Lyon William	Stamford, Broad Street	Stamford	1860	BM			0	0
Manning Alice	Boston, Sibsey Lane	Boston	1812	BM Master	0			
Mason John / Joseph	Grimsby, Upper Burgeholt?	Spalding		BM	0			
Mason William	Grimsby, Upper Burgeholt?	Deeping St James	1811	BM	0			
Mason William	Grimsby, Upper Burgeholt?	Spalding	1846	BM	0	0		
May Amos G	Kirton Lindsey	Kirton Lindsey	1836	BM	0			
May H	Owston Ferry			BM		0		
May Thomas	Kirton Lindsey, Low Town	Scotton	1812	BM	0	0	0	0
Mills George	Grantham, Spittlegate	Somerset, Bath	1858	BM			0	
Milson William	Brigg, Wrawby Street	Brigg	1848	BM			0	0
Milson William	Brigg, Butchery Court	Boston	1794	BM	0	0		
Mitchell Thomas	Grimsby, Bull Ring Ln			BM		0		
Molson -	Boston, James St	Boston	1828	BM	0			
Molson Edwd John	Boston, Pipe Off. Ln	Boston	1844	BM	0		0	
Molson James	Grimsby, Elizabeth Terr.	Boston	1843	BM			0	
Molson Jas Keal	Boston, Pipe Off. Ln	Boston	1842	BM	0			
Molson Samuel	Boston, Pipe Off Ln	Swineshead	1811	BM	0			
Molson Sml Keal	Boston, Pipe Off. Ln	Boston	1831	BM	0			
Molson William J	Grimsby, Dawsons Bldgs	Boston	1833	BM	0		0	
Moor Robert H	Sleaford, South St	Swineshead	1845	BM	0			
Moor Samuel	Sleaford, South St.	Algarkirk	1799	BM	0			
Moore Saml W	Horncastle, Maypole Hill	Swineshead	1828	BM	0			
Morris Thomas	Sleaford / Manthorpe	Sleaford	1832	BM	0	0	0	
Mould John	Stamford, North St	Northants, ?thorpe	1810	BM	0			
Moulson Johnson	Boston, Petticoat Ln	Swineshead	1807	BM	0			
Munday William	Stamford / Heckington	Stamford	1845	BM appr	0			0
Murphy Edward	Grimsby, Thesiger Street	Grimsby	1863	BM			0	
Norris Edward	Boston, Bridge St	Boston	1809	BM	0			
Norris Fredk (son)	Boston, Bridge St	Boston	1837	BM	0			
Norton Walter	Grimsby, Bridge Street	Suffolk, Honington	1855	BM			0	

Lincolnshire basket makers - 1850 - 1900
(Sourced from Census 1861 and 1881 and Trade directories from 1872 and 1889).

Name	Address	Birthplace	Birth	BM Detail	1861	1872	1881	1889
Osbourne John	Lincoln, High Street	N. Somercotes	1836	BM			0	0
Owen Richard	Lincoln, High Street	Lincoln	1808	BM	0			
Parker John	Grimsby, Wellowgate	Yorks, Hull	1837	BM			0	
Parnell Charles	Grimsby, Ravenspurn St	Norfolk, Norwich	1846	BM			0	
Parnell James	Grimsby, Ravenspurn St	Norfolk, Yarmouth	1865	BM			0	
Pask William	Spalding, Broad St			BM				0
Patrick Samuel	Lincoln, High Street	Stamford	1820	Master BM Empl.	0	0	0	
Phillips James	Grimsby, Atkinsons Houses	Boston	1841	BM			0	
Phillips Joseph.	Boston, Wormgate	Boston	1809	BM	0		0	0
Pick James	Carlton Scroop	Carlton Scroop	1809	BM (blind)	0	0	0	
Pocklington William	Long Sutton, Clement Terr			BM/Scuttle mkr			0	
Price James	Manthorpe, Malt Hill	Warw, Leamington	1856	BM			0	
Pullen Richard H	Grimsby, Macaulay St	Yorks, Hull	1848	BM			0	
Pycroft F	Crowland, Reform St			BM		0		
Ratcliffe Annie	Stamford, Red Lion Square	Northampton	1840	BM			0	0
Ratcliffe William	Stamford, Red Lion St	Stamford	1835	BM	0	0		
Rhyder John	Spittlegate, Cambridge St	Yorks, Pontefract	1842	BM			0	
Roberts Geo. Frank	Gainsbor, Market Place	Notts, Gringley	1860	BM & Shopkpr.			0	
Robertson William	Grantham, Castlegate	Scotland, Nairn	1860	BM			0	
Robinson John	Lincoln, Chapel Ln	Bardney	1831	BM	0			
Robinson Thomas	Grantham, Westgate	Grantham	1801	BM (blind)	0			
Roughton Charles	Stamford, Back St West	Spalding	1795	BM	0			
Ryther John	Grantham, Barrowby Ln	Yorks, Pontefract	1833	BM	0			
Salter Wm J	Boston, West St	Spilsby	1839	BM	0			0
Sewards Charles	Dunston	Northum, Tynemouth	1817	BM (blind)			0	
Shankster George	Grimsby, Victoria Street	Grimsby	1864	BM			0	
Sharp Henry	Grimsby, King Edwd St	Rutland, Barleythorpe	1836	BM	0		0	
Shelbourn Halford	Manthorpe, Vere St	Northants, Helpston	1861	BM			0	
Shepherd Lewis	Messingham, Butt Rd	-	1825	BM			0	
Shipside Edward	Manthorpe, Charles St	Basford	1851	BM			0	
Sissons John	Grimsby, Bethlehem St	Worksop	1824	BM	0			
Smith Henry	Horncastle, St Lawrence Ln	Horncastle	1813	BM	0			
Smith John	Grimsby, Hayes Gardens	Yorks, Hull	1844	BM	0			
Snart Henry	Metheringham, Middle St	Rutland, Ketton	1802	BM	0			
Snart Mary A	Manthorpe, Sydney St	Boston	1842	BM wife			0	
Snart R	Bourne, Church St			BM		0		
Snart Thomas D.S	Manthorpe, Sydney St	Lincoln	1846	BM			0	
Spashett Herbert	Clee, Victor Street	Grimsby	1867	BM			0	
Speechly John C	Manthorpe, New Street	Grantham	1865	BM			0	
Spicer Matthew	Gainsborough, Church St	Gainsborough	1825	BM & Cooper	0	0	0	0
Sprawson Walter	Manthorpe, Malt Hill	Birmingham	1856	BM			0	

Lincolnshire basket makers - 1850 - 1900
(Sourced from Census 1861 and 1881 and Trade directories from 1872 and 1889).

Name	Address	Birthplace	Birth	BM Detail	1861	1872	1881	1889
Stanger Charles	Stamford, Broad St	Lincoln	1844	BM	0		0	
Steel Geo William	Grimsby, Old Bridge Terr.	Yorks, Goole	1860	BM			0	
Stevenson Thomas	Manthorpe, James Street	Grantham	1863	BM			0	
Stubbins Charles	Broughton, Bridge Street	Broughton	1811	BM		0	0	0
Stubbins Thomas M.	Broughton, Bridge Street	Brigg	1860	BM			0	
Swift T	Metheringham			BM		0		
Tabor George J	Mkt Deeping/Spalding Workh.	Cambs, March	1811	Pauper, was BM			0	
Taylor Henry	Gainsborough, Caskgate	Gainsborough	1851	BM		0	0	0
Taylor Mary Ann	Gainsborough, Caskgate	Gainsborough	1823	BM			0	
Temperton? Sarah Ann	Stamford, Gas Lane	Boston	1843	BM	0			
Thorpe Gilbert	Ingham			BM		0		
Thorpe John	Ingham	Ingham	1820	BM (blind)			0	
Tilford John	Manthorpe, Manners St	Basford	1855	BM			0	
Truswell Thomas	Louth, Brackenborough Ln	Chilwell	1836	BM			0	
Urry Jesse	Market Rasen, King St	Grimsby	1833	BM	0		0	
Vincent William S	Manthorpe, Vere Street	Warw. Birmingham	1864	BM			0	
Ward Richard	Boston, off Blue St	Kirton, Boston	1837	BM (blind)	0			
Webster George	Grimsby, Pinfold Hill	Grimsby	1843	BM	0			
White Frederick	Holbeach, Church Street	Cambs, March	1854	Master BM			0	0
Whiting Charles	Grimsby, Lower Spring St	Yorks, Hull	1798	BM	0			
Wilkinson Thomas	Grimsby, Albert Street	Yorks, Hull	1846	BM			0	
Williams Thomas	Stamford, All Saints Place	Leics, Littlethorpe	1829	BM	0			
Willis George	Barrow on Humber	Sutton on Trent	1849	Willow sorter			0	
Wilson Charles	Gainsborough, Wilson St	Gainsborough	1844	BM	0			
Wilson George C	Gainsborough, Tongs Yd	Gainsborough	1843	BM			0	
Winter Mary	Boston, West Street	Sutton on Trent	1811	BM	0		0	
Winter William	Boston, High St.	Suffolk, Ipswich	1810	BM Master Empl	0			
Wood Ann	Grantham, Westgate	Leics, Bottesford	1824	BM			0	0
Wood Arthur Leighton	Grantham, Westgate	Grantham	1866	BM			0	
Wood Charles	Grantham, Wharf Rd			BM		0		
Wood Fred C Joseph	Grantham, Westgate	Grantham	1857	BM			0	
Wood Stephen	Grantham, Wharf Rd	Grantham	1825	BM Master	0	0		
Wood William	Manthorpe, North Street	Grantham	1818	BM			0	
Wood William	Grantham, Westgate	Norwell	1786	BM	0			
Wright Charles	Lincoln, Waterside South	Lincoln	1821	Master BM	0	0	0	0
Wright John W.	Lincoln, Pipe Court	Lincoln	1853	Master BM			0	
Wright Phillip	Lincoln, High Street	Lincoln	1847	BM appr	0			
Younger Erdley Willow	Alford, South Bridge	Spilsby	1845	BM	0			
Younger Robert	Alford, South Bridge	Hogsthorpe	1821	BM	0	0	0	0
Younger Samuel	Alford, South Bridge	Spilsby	1847	BM	0			
Younger Willie	Alford, South Parade	Alford	1863	BM			0	

Lincolnshire basket makers 1905 - 1937 - sourced from Trade directories

Name	Location	Address	Occ detail	1905	1919	1926	1937
Aistrup Thomas	Spalding		BM	0	0	0	0
Barratt Henry	Bourne		BM	0			
Barrick John	Barrow on Humber		BM	0			
Bedford Wm	Long Sutton		BM	0			
Belton Francis	Horncastle		BM	0			
Boswell B	Louth		BM		0	0	
Boswell James	Louth		BM	0			
Bowens Joseph	Boston	Wormgate	BM	0			
British Basket Co Ltd	Long Sutton		BM				0
Brown Edward	Horncastle		BM	0			
Burrows Mrs Maria	Lincoln	St Mary's Street	BM	0			
Burton Thos	Sutton Bridge		BM			0	0
Clark John	Scunthorpe		BM	0			
Clark John Wm	Hogsthorpe		BM			0	0
Clements Mrs Sarah A	Boston	West St	BM	0			
Cobley John W	Grimsby	Kent Street	BM	0			
Colbeck George	Louth	Ashley Road	BM				0
Cooling Alfred	Metheringham		BM	0			
Coppin Harry	Louth	Eastgate	BM		0		
Coppin John	Louth		BM	0			
Donner Wm	Barrow on Humber		BM	0			
Dowse Wm	Louth & Spilsby		BM	0			
Drakes Thos	Grimsby	Victoria St	BM	0	0		
Drakes Thos Jnr	Grimsby	Fish Dock Rd	BM	0			
Fish George	Owston Ferry		BM	0	0		
Fish Iram	Owston Ferry		BM			0	0
Fitzpatrick Bernard	Grimsby	Fish Dock, Freeman St	BM			0	
Friend Chas Wm	Stamford	Broad St	BM		0	0	0
Fuller H	Grimsby	Cartergate	BM			0	0
Fuller J	Grimsby	New Cartergate	BM				0
Gale & Sons	Gainsborough	Bridge St	BM			0	
Genney Wm	Grimsby	Fish Dock Rd	BM	0			
Gilchrist Chas R	Boston	Queen St	BM		0	0	0
Hall Thos	Crowland		BM	0			
Harris & Son	Grimsby	Abbey Walk	BM	0	0	0	0
Harrison Wm	Sleaford & Grantham		BM/Furn Manuf	0	0	0	0
Ireland George W	Grimsby	Cleethorpes Rd	BM	0			
Islip John	Market Rasen		BM	0			

Lincolnshire basket makers 1905 - 1937 - sourced from Trade directories

Name	Location	Address	Occ detail	1905	1919	1926	1937
Johnson J. Osbourne	Brant Broughton	Meeting House Lane	BM				0
Kirk Joseph	Lincoln	New Mkt & Steep Hill	BM	0			
Knight Wm	Louth		BM	0			
Latter Hy	Gt Gonerby		BM		0		
Lyon Mrs Mary	Stamford	Broad St	BM	0			
Mackinder Harry	Spilsby		BM		0	0	
May Thos	Kirton Lindsey		BM		0		
Milson Wm	Brigg		BM		0		
Mitchell George	Grimsby	Bull Ring Lane	BM		0		
Munday Wm	Heckington		BM		0		
Osborne John	Lincoln	Broadgate	BM		0	0	
Osborne TW & Sons	Lincoln	Broadgate	BM			0	
Patrick Richard	Lincoln	High St	BM	0			
Pearce Stephen	Woolsthorpe		BM				0
Pearson Herbert	Grimsby	Lord St	BM				0
Ratcliffe Mrs Annie	Stamford	Red Lion St	BM	0			
Salter Wm	Boston	George St	BM	0	0		
Sharpe Wm	Grantham	Comm. Rd & Church. St	BM	0	0	0	
Smith Wm	Lincoln	Oxford St	BM	0			
Spicer Matthew	Gainsborough		BM	0			
Stafford Geo	Bourne	Market Place	BM		0	0	0
Stamp Wm Henry	Boston	Wormgate	BM		0	0	0
Stubbins Charles	Brigg		BM	0			
Taylor H & E	Gainsborough		BM	0			
Tomlinson R	Market Rasen		BM	0			
Walker Mrs Elizabeth	Boston	Wormgate	BM	0			
West Herbert	Louth	Market Hall	BM		0	0	0
White Frederick	Holbeach		BM		0	0	
Whittaker Edward	Sleaford		BM	0			
Wood Arthur	Grantham	Westgate	BM	0			
Wood Mrs Emma	Grantham	Wharf Rd	BM	0			
Woods Frederick	Grantham	Bridge St	BM	0			
Wright JD	Spalding	Double St	BM		0	0	0
Wright Thomas	Spalding	Double St	BM	0			
Wright & Son	Lincoln	Waterside South	BM		0	0	0
Younger Eardley	Alford	Market Place	BM	0			
Younger Robert	Alford		BM	0			

Lincolnshire Adverts

THIS IS THE WORK OF

J. O. JOHNSON
Blind Basket Maker
MEETING HOUSE LANE
BRANT BROUGHTON, Nr. LINCOLN

You'll find many purposes for which
Basketwork is the Best
it is Light, Strong and Durable

Here are a few examples and Prices:

SHOPPING BASKETS	Oblong		..	12/-
,,	,,	Deep	..	14/6
,,	,,	Kiddies' Size	..	6/-
CLOTHES	,,	Medium	..	20/-
,,	,,	Large	..	26/-
WASTEPAPER	,,		..	17/-
FISHING	,,		..	42/-
SEWING	,,		..	19/-
PICNIC	,,		..	32/-
LUNCH	,,		..	17/-
CYCLE	,,		..	13/6
PRAM	,,		..	17/-
PET	,,		..	21/-

and of course many more
(Prices are approximate)
For any further details just send a postcard
And don't forget where the occasion calls for
a present maybe I can help
(All prices shown are for the standard
size basket delivered to Lincoln)

P.T.O.

An advertising flyer for J. Osbourne Johnson of Brant Broughton, 1930s

---

W. MUNDAY, Jun.,
BASKET, SCUTTLE & SIEVE MAKER,
SCOTGATE, STAMFORD,

Begs respectfully to inform the Inhabitants of Stamford and neighbourhood that he has commenced in the above business, and hopes by unremitting attention to all orders, combined with first-class workmanship, to merit a share of their patronage and support.

Bassinetts, Cradles, Children's Chairs, and all kinds of Fancy Baskets. Cane Work, and Repairs neatly executed.

CARRIAGE BODIES MADE TO ORDER.

W. Munday of Stamford. Advert from Morris's Trade Directory, 1866.

36, Broad Street,
Stamford, _____ 1902

M __ Dr Eddows

Bought of WILLIAM LYON,
Basket, Scuttle, Skep, Sieve and Hamper Maker.

Copy of an invoice of William Lyon of Stamford, a family with a long basket making tradition. In 1735, a poor child of Stamford was apprenticed to a John Lyon the elder. Lincolnshire Archives ref 13/2/5

Iram and fellow basket making Yellerbellies

Iram Hill, basket maker of Owston Ferry. Photo from Owston Ferry Museum.

ROBERT YOUNGER,
BASKET, RIDDLE, & SCUTTLE MAKER,
AND CANE-WORKER,
SOUTH BRIDGE, ALFORD.

PERAMBULATORS AND BASKET CARRIAGES,
MADE TO ORDER.
Sieves, Brushes, Pails, and Tubs.

Advert from Morris's Commercial Trade Directory Lincolnshire 1863

G. MITCHELL & CO.,
Basket ✢ Makers, ✢ Coopers,
— AND —
GENERAL DEALERS.
ROPE, TWINE & BRUSH WAREHOUSE.
FARMERS' WORK KEPT IN STOCK.
Chairs Re-seated & Fancy Work Neatly Repaired.
ALL ORDERS RECEIVE PROMPT ATTENTION.
Old Market Place (Works: BETHLEHEM STREET), GRIMSBY.

Advert from Kelly's Directory Lincolnshire 1896

A Basketful

Nottinghamshire basket makers pre 1851, sourced from Trade directories

Name	Address	BM detail	1829	1832	1835	1841	1848
Andrews Margaret	Newark, Wilson Street	BM			0		
Barker John	Nottm, Greyhound St	BM	0	0	0	0	
Barker Samuel	Nottm, Greyhound St	BM	0				
Barlow Thos	Carlton, Nottingham	BM			0		
Bates Ann	Newark, Wilson Street	BM	0	0			
Bates, John	Newark, Wilson Street	BM	0	0	0		
Beedham Thomas	East Stoke	BM appr	0				
Beeston John	Blyth	BM				0	0
Bettison Wm	Retford, Bridgegate	BM	0	0	0	0	0
Blower John	East Stoke	BM				0	
Brewell Edward	East Stoke	BM appr				0	
Burton Thomas	Carlton, Nottingham	BM		0			
Clarke James	Newark, Lombard Street	BM	0	0	0	0	
Clayton James	Nottm, Sheep Lane	BM		0	0	0	
Clayton John	Nottm, Derby Road	BM	0	0		0	
Clayton Joseph	Nottm, Greyhound Yard	BM	0	0			
Cockayne John	Hyson Green, Nottingham	BM					0
Cowlishaw Jonathan	Gedling	BM					0
Cowlishaw Wm	Carlton, Nottingham	BM					0
Cowlishaw Wm	Gedling	BM					0
Cowlishaw Wm	East Stoke	BM			0		
Dallaway R	Southwell, Back Lane	BM			0		
Felston John	Nottingham, Low Pavement	BM	0				
Flint Wm	Worksop, Potter Street	BM	0	0	0	0	0
Franks Richard	Newark, Boar Lane	BM				0	0
Garth John	Newark, Lombard Street	BM					0
Gee Francis	East Stoke	BM			0	0	0
Gilbert John	Nottm, Hollowstone	BM				0	
Glew John	Radford, Elliott St	BM					0
Griffin Richard	Sneinton, Nottingham	BM	0				
Griffith Elizabeth	Newark, Castle Gate	BM	0				
Halifax Wm	Warsop	BM			0		0
Holliday John	Retford, Spa Lane	BM	0	0	0	0	0
Horsley Edward	Carlton, Nottingham	BM			0	0	
James Charles	Mansfield, Clarkson's Alley	BM				0	0
James Oliver	Mansfield, Leeming Street	BM			0	0	
Meakin John	Radford, Princes Street	BM					0
Merrin Elizabeth	Nottm, Hollowstone	BM	0	0	0		
Merrin Robert	Wilford	BM					0
Mills John & Wm	East Leake	BM			0		0
Mills William	West Leake	BM					0
Musson John	Barton in Fabis	BM					0

Nottinghamshire basket makers pre 1851, sourced from Trade directories

Name	Address	BM detail	1829	1832	1835	1841	1848
North John	Newark, Castle Gate	BM	0	0	0	0	0
Padgett Thomas	East Stoke	BM				0	
Parson George	Warsop	BM					0
Parsons John	Worksop, Market Place	BM	0	0	0		0
Perkins Wm	Sherwood, Nottingham	BM					0
Phillips John	Newark, Carter Gate	BM	0			0	0
Pocklington David	Newark, Mill Gate	BM	0				
Rawson John	East Stoke	BM		0		0	0
Rawson Thomas	Southwell, Easthorpe	BM	0	0		0	0
Richmond John	Cromwell	BM		0			0
Richmond Thomas	Retford	BM/Cooper					0
Roe William	Nottm, Virginia Street	BM			0	0	
Roulstone David	Radcliffe on Trent	BM				0	
Roulstone John	Radcliffe on Trent	BM				0	0
Roulstone Wm Snr	Radcliffe on Trent	BM				0	0
Roulstone Wm Jnr	Radcliffe on Trent	BM				0	
Scotney Shelton	Nottingham, Goosegate	BM				0	
Smart Thomas	Nottingham, Fisher Gate	BM				0	
Smith Henry	Nottingham, Fisher Gate	BM			0		
Smith James	Nottingham, Wheeler Gate	BM/Matter				0	0
Smith John	Nottingham, Fisher Gate	BM	0				
Smith Joseph	Nottingham, Fisher Gate	BM				0	
Southern Reuben	Bingham, Union St	BM					0
Stott John	Nottingham, Rigley's Yd	BM				0	
Watts Henry & Sons	Nottingham, Angel Row	BM	0	0	0	0	
Withers Wm John Boot	Ratcliffe on Soar	BM			0		0

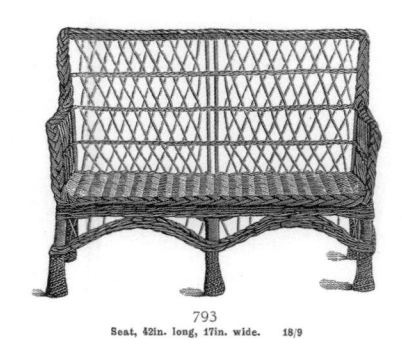

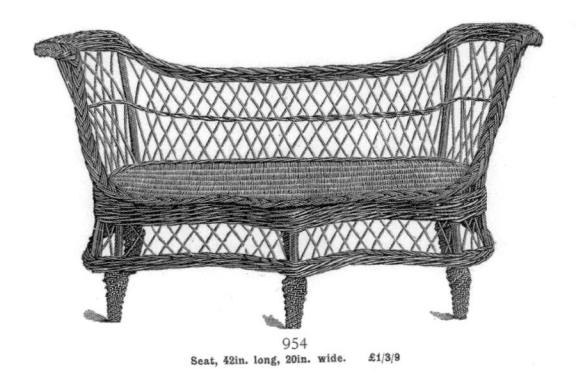

Illustrations from Harrison's of Grantham 'Artistic Willow' catalogue, 1912.

A Basketful

Nottinghamshire basket makers 1851 - 1891 from Census Returns
(Birth years are approximate)

Name	Address	Occ detail	Birthplace	Year	1851	1861	1871	1881	1891
Allen Elijah	Bulwell, Hayfield Ln	BM	Bulwell	1854				0	0
Allen Elizabeth	Lenton, Tyne St	BM	Bingham	1852				0	
Allen John	Lenton, Tyne St	BM	Sleaford	1844				0	
Andrews Thomas	Newark, Portland Street	BM appr	Newark	1879					0
Askew Samuel	Warsop	BM	Boughton	1840		0	0	0	0
Askew Thomas	Warsop, High Street	BM	Warsop	1870					0
Atkinson George	Southwell, Back Lane	BM	Basford	1855					0
Barker Frank	Bingham, Newgate St	BM	Bingham	1862				0	
Barker Wm	Lowdham	BM	Nottingham	1821				0	
Barlow Harriet	Farndon	Osier Peeler	Waddington	1833					0
Barnes John	Shelford	BM	Shelford	1827	0	0	0		0
Barnes Joseph	Farndon	BM	York	1845				0	
Barratt Eliza	Sutton in Ashfield	BM	Sutton in Ashfield	1838				0	
Barratt John	Retford, Spa Lane	BM	Lincoln	1803			0		
Barratt William	Sutton in Ashfield	BM	Mansfield	1841				0	
Barrett Thomas	Retford	BM	Lincoln	1802	0				
Barton Henry	Retford	BM	Newark	1811	0	0	0		
Bates John	Newark	BM Retired	Newark	1772	0				
Baxter John	Lenton, Salisbury St	BM	Nottingham	1848				0	
Beaumont Wm	Collingham, Cabbage Row	BM	Spridlington	1858				0	
Beckitt William	Newark, Barnby Gate	BM	Newark	1829					0
Beedham Anthony	Newark, Eggleston's Yd	BM	Bassingham	1843			0		
Beedon George	Collingham	BM	Elston	1853				0	
Beedon Thomas	Thorpe	BM	Willoughby, Lincs	1826	0	0	0		
Beeston John	Blyth	BM	East Stoke	1813				0	
Beeston Richard	Worksop	BM	Blyth	1850				0	
Bell Emma	Southwell, Kirklington Rd	Rod Peeler	Farndon	1867					0
Bell George	Southwell, Westgate	BM	Southwell	1861					0
Bell John	Southwell, Westgate	Basket worker	Southwell	1869					0
Bell Mary E	Southwell, Westgate	Basket worker	Southwell	1870					0
Bettison William	Retford, Bridgegate	BM/Cooper, 7 men	Retford	1815	0	0	0		
Bickett Wm A	Newark, Barnby Gate	BM	Newark	1831				0	
Bingham Richard	Newark, Regent Street	BM	Northants, Deeping	1831		0	0		
Blatherwick Thomas	Saxondale	BM	Gunthorpe	1762	0				
Blower John	East Stoke	BM	Derbys, Ticknall	1816	0	0	0	0	
Boothby Henry	Retford, Spa Lane	BM	Boston	1825			0		
Boothby Henry	Ordsall	BM	Boston	1833				0	
Braisby Benjamin	Plumtree	BManuf.	Leics, Wymeswold	1846				0	0
Brake Martin	Southwell, Easthorpe	BM appr	Dorset, Lyme Regis	1878					0

68   A Basketful

Nottinghamshire basket makers 1851 - 1891 from Census Returns
(Birth years are approximate)

Name	Address	Occ detail	Birthplace	Year	1851	1861	1871	1881	1891
Brewill Edward	Newark	BM Journeyman	East Stoke	1827	0				
Brooks George	Nottm, Corporation Rd	Wicker Worker	Oxford	1855				0	
Brooks Wm	Newark, Portland St	BM	Bristol	1848				0	
Brown George	Ordsall	BM	Retford	1849			0		
Brown Henry	Retford	BM & Cooper	Retford	1848				0	
Bucklow John	Nottm, Earnshaw Yd	BM	Southwell	1842				0	
Buckton John	Southwell, Easthorpe	BM appr	Southwell	1842			0		
Bullivant Samuel	Nottm, Galloway's Yd	BM	Nottingham	1854				0	
Burton William	Bulwell, Powis St	BM	Bulwell	1849				0	
Buxton Wm	Bulwell, Latimer St	BM	Bulwell	1856				0	
Camomile Daniel	Cromwell	BM appr	Cromwell	1832	0				
Capson John	Newark, Eldon Street	BM	Nottingham	1841			0		
Capson Samuel	Southwell, Westgate	BM	Nottingham	1854					0
Cartwright George	Newark, Bradley's Yd	BM	Yorks. Hull	1847			0		
Caunt John	Bingham	BM appr	Hickling	1848			0		
Chambers Phillip	Bulwell, Duchess St	BM	Cinderhill	1858				0	
Chapman John	Retford	BM	Lincoln	1804			0	0	
Chapman John	Newark, Kirk Gate	BM	Lincoln	1804			0		
Clay Alfred	Farndon	BM	Bulwell	1858				0	
Clayton Frederick	Nottm, Parliament St	BM	Nottingham	1827				0	
Clayworth Caroline	Newark, Clarke's Yd	Rod Peeler	Newark	1831			0		
Cobham Robert	Farndon	BM	Lancs, Mawdesley	1840			0	0	0
Dickenson William	Styrrup	BM (blind)	Styrrup	1861				0	
Dixon George	Southwell, Kirklington Rd	Rod Peeler	Farnsfield	1878					0
Dixon John W	Southwell, Easthorpe	BM	Farndon	1871					0
Dixon Mary	Southwell, Kirklington Rd	Rod Peeler	Farndon	1852					0
Dixon Wm	Retford	BM	Laxton	1828				0	
Elam John	Newark, Castle Gate	BM *Empl 2m 1b	Horncastle	1850				0	
Elam Martha	Newark, London Road	Basket Vendor	Kirkstead	1851					0
Elliott Henry	Mansfield, Botany	Wicker BM	Norfolk, Stalham	1853				0	
Foster Eliza	Lowdham	BM	Lowdham	1868					0
Foster Elizabeth	Retford, Chancery Lane	BM	Retford	1839		0			
Foster George	Southwell, King Street	BM	London	1869					0
Foster George W	Southwell, Westhorpe	BM appr	Southwell	1873					0
Foster Topes?	Retford, Chancery Lane	BM	Newark	1838		0			
Franks Ambrose	Newark, Carter Gate	BM	Nottingham	1865				0	
Franks Charles	Newark, Carter Gate	BM	Newark	1840				0	
Franks Elizabeth	Newark, Boar Lane	BM	Newark	1802		0			
Franks John	Newark, Boar Lane	BM	Dunham	1828	0	0	0		

Nottinghamshire basket makers 1851 - 1891 from Census Returns
(Birth years are approximate)

Name	Address	Occ detail	Birthplace	Year	1851	1861	1871	1881	1891
Franks John	Newark, Middle Gate	BM	Newark ?	1834				0	
Franks Richard	Newark, Boar Lane	BM empl 4 men	Newark 1802	1795	0				
Gascoigne John	Southwell, Kirklington Rd	Rod Mercht's Lab.	Southwell	1867					0
Gascoigne William	Southwell, Kirklington Rd	BM	Southwell	1869					0
Gee Francis	East Stoke	BM	East Stoke	1794	0				
Griffin William	Radford, Forster St	BM	Leics, Shepshed	1831				0	
Griffith Joseph	Basford, Chapel St.	BM	Wilford	1804	0				
Groves Thomas	Retford	BM	Mattersey	1788	0				
Halifax John	Warsop	BM	Warsop	1802		0			
Halifax John	Warsop	BM empl 1m	Warsop	1843		0	0	0	
Halifax Mary	Warsop	BM wife	Norwell	1801		0			
Halifax Mary	Warsop	BM wife	Mansfield	1831		0			
Halifax Sarah	Warsop	BM dau.	Warsop	1839		0			
Halifax William	Warsop	BM	Warsop	1829	0	0			
Halifax William	Warsop	BM empl 2men	Warsop	1779	0				
Hardstaff Thomas	Nottm, Portland Rd	Com.Trav (Baskets)	Linby	1840				0	
Hardy Thomas	Collingham	BM	Yorks. Hull	1847				0	
Harrison Joseph	Southwell, Easthorpe	BM	Derbys, Sawley	1820	0	0	0		
Hazard Ann	Cromwell	Rod Peeler	Norwell	1843		0			
Hazlewood Robert	Southwell, Easthorpe	BM	Yorks, Selby	1862					0
Hedge William	Southwell, Easthorpe	BM appr	Barton in Fabis	1847			0		
Herrod Wm	Farndon	Willow grower	Farndon	1818				0	
Hickinbottham Thos.	Southwell, King Street	BM	Leics, Cas. Donington.	1862					0
Hind Samuel	Southwell, King Street	Rod Buffer	Mansfield	1876					0
Hodson Elizabeth	Lenton, Park Place	BM	Ilkeston	1851				0	
Hodson John	Lenton, Park Place	BM	Lancs, Preston	1847				0	
Holland Francis	Arnold, High St	BM	Costock	1826				0	
Holliday Edward	Retford, Carolgate	BM appr	Retford	1835	0				
Holliday Edward	Clarborough							0	
Holliday John	Retford, Carolgate	BM	Retford	1808	0		0	0	0
Howett Jane	Radford, Greek St	BM	Leicester	1863				0	
Howett Thomas	Radford, Greek St	BM	Willoughby, Notts	1828				0	
Hudson William	Southwell, King street	Rod Buffer	Derby	1862					0
James Charles	Mansfield, Clarkson's Alley	Master BM	Mansfield	1799	0				
James Jacob	Mansfield, Clarkson's Alley	BM	Mansfield	1801	0				
James John	Mansfield, Clarkson's Alley	BM	Sheffield	1833	0				
Jepson Eliza	Southwell, Westgate	Rod Buffer	Southwell	1878					0
Jepson Emma	Southwell, Westgate	Rod Buffer	Southwell	1876					0
Johnson James	Newark, Eldon Street	BM	Southport	1844			0		

70   A Basketful

Nottinghamshire basket makers 1851 - 1891 from Census Returns
(Birth years are approximate)

Name	Address	Occ detail	Birthplace	Year	1851	1861	1871	1881	1891
Kemp James	Nottingham, James Street	BM	Leicester	1827				0	
Kemp James	Nottingham, James Street	BM	Northampton	1854				0	
Knowles Henry	Radford, Chapel St	BM	Kimberley	1821				0	
Knowles Sarah	Radford, Chapel St	BM	Bilborough	1848				0	
Levi Henry John	Radcliffe	BM	Nottingham	1838		0			
Lewers Geo Henry	Bulwell, Basford Rd	BM	Bulwell	1852				0	
Longbottom Frank	Southwell, Easthorpe	BM appr	Farndon	1876					0
Longbottom Joseph	Southwell, Easthorpe	BM	Farndon	1874					0
Makin Henry	Warsop, High Street	BM appr	Warsop	1853			0		
Marshall John	Southwell, Burgage	BM	Gringley on the Hill	1874					0
Mayfield Joseph	Shelford	BM	Cromwell	1785	0				
Meakin Sarah	Newark, Middle Gate	BM	Newark	1842					0
Measham Richard	Southwell, Kirklington Rd	BM	Leics Ashby/Zouch	1872					0
Measham William	Southwell, Kirklington Rd	BM	Derbys, Repton	1839					0
Merrin Hannah	Wilford	BM wife	Aslockton	1815		0			
Merrin Robert	Wilford	BM	Wilford	1814	0	0	0		
Middleton Herbert	Bulwell, Edith Terr.	BM	Bulwell	1866				0	
Mills Augustus	Southwell, Westgate	BM	East Leake	1874					0
Mills John	Newark, North Gate	BM	Leics, Bergholt	1814			0		
Mills John Horace	Southwell, Kirklington Rd	Willow Merchant	East Leake	1857					0
Moore Harry	Southwell, Back Lane	BM appr	Southwell	1875					0
Morley Thomas	Newark, Old Lock House	BM	Barton in Fabis	1811		0			
Morley Thomas	Newark, Castle Gate	BM	Balderton?	1811	0				
Morris Thomas	Nottingham, Birkland Ave	Manager B W'ho.	Tollerton	1861				0	
Morris William	Wilford	BM	Wilford	1827			0		
Nawton Francis	Worksop	BM & Cooper	Yorks, Ampleforth	1807				0	
Nawton Francis W	Worksop	BM & Cooper	Worksop	1837				0	
Newham John	Gunthorpe, Nottm	BM	Gunthorpe	1813				0	
Newton Harriet	Farndon	Rod Peeler	Farndon	1841					0
Nickels John	Clarborough	BM	Norfolk, Stalham	1841		0		0	
Nickels John	Thorpe, Holt House	BM	Norfolk, E Ruston?	1841				0	
Noakes William	Southwell, Kirklington Rd	BM Manager	London	1862					0
North Elizabeth	Newark, Castle Gate	BM	Newark	1786			0		
North John	Newark, Castle Gate	BM empl 5 men	Newark	1786	0	0			
Oldham Walter	Bulwell, Latimer St	BM	Bulwell	1867				0	
Osborne John	Bulwell, Hayfield Ln	BM	Bulwell	1852				0	
Pallant John	Newark, Water Lane	BM	Suffolk	1781	0				
Parker Henry	Radcliffe	BM	Radcliffe	1845			0		
Parkinson Thomas	Worksop, Cheapside	BM	Retford/Gainsbor.	1788	0	0			

Nottinghamshire basket makers 1851 - 1891 from Census Returns
(Birth years are approximate)

Name	Address	Occ detail	Birthplace	Year	1851	1861	1871	1881	1891
Parr David	Lowdham	Willow Peeler	Lowdham	1877					0
Parson George	Warsop, Carr Lane	BM/Farmer	Worksop	1814		0	0		
Parson John	Worksop, Wh. Hart Yd	BM	Worksop	1798	0	0			
Parson Mary	Worksop, Wh. Hart Yd	BM	Worksop	1823	0				
Parson Sarah	Worksop	BM	Wellow?	1800	0				
Peacock Thomas	Southwell, Normanton	BM	Hunts, Kimbolton	1870					0
Pearson Frederick	Nottm. Newcastle Circus	BManuf.	Rutland	1830				0	
Percival Elizabeth	Southwell, Back Lane	Rod Holt Worker	Southwell	1818				0	
Perkins Harriet	Lenton, New Inn Yd	BM	Northants, Oundle	1852				0	
Perkins Robert	Sherwood	BM	Nottingham	1837	0				
Perkins William	Sherwood	BM	Leics, Lutterworth	1802	0		0		
Perkins Wm C	Lenton, New Inn Yd	BM	Nottingham	1851				0	
Pinkett Cornelius	Bulwell, Forest Rd	BM	Bulwell	1860				0	
Plumber John	Wilford	BM appr	Muskham?	1834	0				
Pyband Wm	Nottm, Cumberland Pl	BM	Grantham	1812				0	
Radford John	Bulwell, Hempshill Ln	BM	Bulwell	1860				0	
Raworth Isabella	Southwell, Back Lane	Rod Holt worker	Southwell	1856				0	
Rawson George	Elston	BM *Empl 1m	East Stoke	1836			0	0	0
Rawson George	Barton in Fabis	BM	Barton in Fabis	1826	0				
Rawson Harry/Henry	Elston	BM	East Stoke	1866				0	0
Rawson Henry	Thorpe	Scuttle maker	East Stoke	1836		0			
Rawson John	Elston	BM	East Stoke	1868					0
Rawson John	Thorpe/Elston	BM/Scuttle mkr	East Stoke	1845		0	0	0	0
Rawson John	East Stoke	BM	Barton in Fabis	1788	0	0			
Rawson William	Barton in Fabis	BM	Barton in Fabis	1798	0				
Rayner Frederick	Sneinton, Carlton Rd	BM	Nottingham	1847				0	
Read Henry	Radford, Boden St	BM	Radford	1846				0	
Reede? Thomas	Newark, Boar Lane	BM	N. Muskham	1778	0				
Revell Wm	Bulwell, Hercules Place	BM	Bulwell	1851				0	
Rice George	Barton in Fabis	BM	Barton in Fabis	1844		0		0	0
Richardson Israel	Bingham, Pond St	BM	Wilford	1820		0	0	0	0
Richardson Robert L	Bingham	BM	Bingham	1852			0	0	0
Richardson Sarah	Bingham, Pond St	BM	Redmile	1821				0	
Richmond Charles	Collingham	BM	Cromwell	1809	0				
Richmond Dennis	Cromwell	BM	Cromwell	1838		0			
Richmond George	Cromwell	BM Journeyman	Retford	1839		0			
Richmond John	Cromwell	BM Journeyman	Cromwell	1826	0				
Richmond John	Cromwell	BM with 20 acres	Cromwell	1796	0	0			
Richmond Thomas	Retford	BM & Cooper	Cromwell	1815	0				

Nottinghamshire basket makers 1851 - 1891 from Census Returns
(Birth years are approximate)

Name	Address	Occ detail	Birthplace	Year	1851	1861	1871	1881	1891
Richmond Thomas	Cromwell	Bm appr	Lincoln	1844		0			
Richmond Thos	Southwell, West Gate	BM *Empl 1m	Radcliffe	1839				0	
Rockley John	Radcliffe on Trent	Bm Journeyman	Radcliffe	1820	0				
Roulstone Francis	Radcliffe, Martins Yd	BM	Radcliffe	1814	0	0			
Roulstone George		BM	Radcliffe	1829		0		0	
Roulstone Jane	Radcliffe on Trent	BM wife	Radcliffe	1830	0				
Roulstone John	Radcliffe	BM	Radcliffe	1805	0				
Roulstone Richard	Radcliffe	Journeyman BM	Radcliffe	1835	0				
Roulstone Samuel	Radcliffe, Martins Yd	BM appr	Radcliffe	1846		0			
Roulstone William	Radcliffe	BM/Wesl Preacher	Radcliffe	1774	0				
Roulstone William	Radcliffe	BM appr	Radcliffe	1839	0				
Roulstone William	Radcliffe	Master BM	Radcliffe	1800	0				
Roulstone George	Radcliffe	BM	Radcliffe	1830		0			
Rowland Saml	Bulwell, New Mkt Rd	BM	Basford	1851				0	
Royston Cuthbert	Nottingham, Albert Street	B Manuf.	Norfolk	1823				0	
Royston Elizabeth	Nottingham, Albert Street	B Manuf.	London	1826				0	
Shaw Samuel	Worksop, Lead Hill	BM	Northants, Raunds	1816		0			
Sherif Jane	Newark, Clarke's Yd	Rod Peeler	Newark	1831			0		
Shiverling Cornelius	Newark, Bradley's Yd	BM	Lancs, Southport	1851			0		
Singleton Harry	Newark, Portland Street	BM	Bingham	1864					0
Skinner Thomas	Newark, Mill Gate	BM	Louth	1825			0		
Smith Edward	Newark, Taylor's Yd	BM	Derby	1845			0		
Smith Frederick	Bingham, Union Street	BM	London	1872					0
Smith William	Wilford	BM appr	Nottingham	1841			0		
Smith William	Newark, Castle Gate	BM	Hunts, St Ives	1811	0				
Southern Reuben	Mansfield	BM	Rufford	1815			0	0	
Southern William	Mansfield, Albert Street	BM	Bulwell	1820			0		
Spittlehouse David	Cottam	Rod Cutter	Marton, Lincs	1867					0
Stanley Edward	Southwell, Westgate	Rod Buffer	Yorks, Brotton	1876					0
Stanley Frederick	Southwell, Westgate	Rod Buffer	Yorks, Saltburn	1872					0
Stevenson Agnes	Southwell, Back Lane	Rod Peeler	Southwell	1863					0
Stevenson George	Southwell, Easthorpe	Buff Rod Peeler	Farndon	1855					0
Stevenson John	Southwell, Back Lane	Rod Peeler	Farndon	1863					0
Summers Henry	Newark, Albion Street	BM appr	Newark	1848		0			
Summers Thomas	Newark, Albion Street	BM appr	Newark	1845		0			
Sunburn Henry	Newark, Barnby Gate	BM	Blyth	1856			0	0	0
Surtees Ralph	Nottingham, Trinity Street	BM empl 7m	Northum, Bellingham	1832				0	
Taylor William	Retford, Spa Lane	BM	Leicester	1812		0			
Thompson Geo W	Collingham, Newark Rd	BM Appr.	Collingham	1863				0	

A Basketful 73

Nottinghamshire basket makers 1851 - 1891 from Census Returns

(Birth years are approximate)

Name	Address	Occ detail	Birthplace	Year	1851	1861	1871	1881	1891
Thompson Thomas	Farndon	Willow Merch.appr	Flintham	1844		0			
Thorneley William	Southwell, Kirklington Rd	BM appr	Southwell	1877					0
Thurston James	Worksop	BM	Camb, Cottenham	1834				0	
Toplis George	Nottingham, Peashill Rd	BM	Derbys, Ilkeston	1825				0	
Truman Joseph	Bulwell, Stockwell St	BM	Bulwell	1861				0	
Truswell Thomas	Southwell, Easthorpe	BM	Chilwell	1836			0		
Truswell Thomas	Worksop, Bridge Street	BM	Chilwell	1836		0			
Turlington Samuel	Lenton, Digby St	BM	Leics, Thorpe	1816				0	
Umney Ezekial	Nottingham, Kent Street	BM empl 2m1b	Bucks, Sherrington	1821				0	
Umney Sarah A	Nottingham, Kent Street	Asst BM	Nottingham	1856				0	
Waine James	Nottm, Goosegate	Osier grower	Nottingham	1846				0	
Wallis Edward	Wilford	BM appr	Wilford	1845		0			
Wass Joseph	Upton Workhouse	BM	Leicester	1815				0	
Webb Charles	Worksop, Norfolk St	BM	N'hants, Towcester	1826		0			
Webb Jane E	Worksop, Norfolk St	BM wife	Worksop	1827		0			
Webb William C	Worksop, Lead Hill	BM	N'hants, Greensnorton	1804		0			
Wells Mary	Southwell, Back Lane	Rod Peeler	Southwell	1856					0
Wetherall William	Newark, Chatham Street	BM	N. Muskham	1839		0			
Whitehead Arthur J	Lenton, Elliott St	BM	Radford	1865				0	
Whitehead Joseph	Lenton, Elliott St	BM	Chilwell	1830				0	
Whitworth Edward	Retford, Playhouse Yd	BM	Lancs, Liverpool	1834				0	0
Whitworth Edward	Ordsall, Albert Rd	BM	Lancs, Liverpool	1834			0		
Widdowson George	Southwell, Easthorpe	BM appr	Southwell	1845		0			
Wilkinson Wm	Wilford	BM	Wilford	1818	0	0	0	0	
Willis John	East Stoke	BM appr	Elston	1833	0				
Willis John	Newark, Eldon St	BM	Elston	1833			0	0	
Willis Robert	Newark, Eldon St.	BM	Norwell	1855				0	0
Wood Alfred	Newark, Crescent Place	BM appr	Newark	1846			0		
Wood Henry	Southwell, Back Lane	BM	Southwell	1872					0
Wood William	Newark, Cherry Holt Lane	BM	Grantham	1818	0	0	0		
Woodward Ernest B	Nottingham, Woodland Pl	BM	Nottingham	1864				0	
Woodward Thomas	Nottingham, Woodland Pl	BM appr	Nottingham	1868				0	
Woodward Thomas	Nottingham, Woodland Pl	BM empl 2m2b	Leicester	1836				0	
Wylde Wm	Woodborough, Calverton Ln	BM (blind)	Woodborough	1853				0	

20th Century Nottinghamshire basket makers sourced from Trade directories

Name	Address	BM detail	1908	1922	1936	1949	1957
Albert Wicker Manuf. Co	Nottingham, Nottm Road	Wicker Furn. Manuf		0			
Askew Samuel	Warsop	Basket maker	0				
Barnes Thos & A	Basford, High Street	Basket maker	0	0		0	
Barnsdale, Bexon & Co	Arnold, Redhill	Wicker Furn. Manuf	0				
Beeston Charles	Blyth	Basket maker		0	0	0	
Beeston John Henry	Blyth	Basket maker	0				
British Basket Works	Nottingham, Lily Street	Basket makers		0	0	0	0
British Cane Splitting Co	Nottingham, Meadow Lane,	Wicker Furn. Manuf		0			
Brooks William	Nottingham, Player Street	Wicker Furn. Manuf	0				
Brown Elijah	Radford, Baldwin Street	Basket maker	0				
Bucklow Frank	Nottingham, Roden Street	Basket maker		0	0	0	0
Bucklow John	Nottingham, Roden Street	Basket maker	0				
Bullivant Samuel & Son	Nottingham, Canal Street	Basket maker	0	0	0	0	
Buxton Hedley	Bulwell, Chatham Street	Basket maker				0	
Buxton William	Bulwell, Chatham Street	Basket maker	0	0		0	
Camm Percy Ltd	Basford, Queen Street	Wicker Furn. Manuf		0	0		
Clark F & Co	Basford, Chelmsford Road	Basket makers	0				
Craddock Thomas P	Newark, Lincoln Road	Basket maker	0	0	0		
Day Edward A	Basford, Elite Works	Wicker Furn. Manuf	0	0	0	0	
Dicks Herbert	Basford, Jasmine Road	Wicker Furn. Manuf	0			0	
Ellis George	Basford, Wycliffe Street	Wicker Furn. Manuf	0				
Frettingham G	Nottingham, Milton Street	Basket maker	0				
Gale Herbert	Beckingham	BM & grower				0	
Grogan Arthur	Nottingham, Carter Gate	Basket maker	0				
Hall George	Nottingham, Mount Street	Basket maker	0				
Hardstaff Thomas	Nottingham, Canal Street	Wicker Furn. Manuf	0	0			
Heaton George	Basford, Mount Pleasant	Wicker Furn. Manuf	0				
Hewson B & Co	Daybrook, Mansfield Road	Wicker Furn. Manuf	0				
Holroyd James A	Basford, High Street	Wicker Furn. Manuf	0				
Hooks Harry	Basford, Wilton Street	Wicker Furn. Manuf	0				
Hoole John	Basford, Olive Square	Basket maker	0				
Hoveringham Basket Co	Lowdham, Cliff Mill	Wicker Furn. Manuf			0	0	
Hudson & Russell	Nottingham, Mount Street	Basket maker	0	0	0		
Ireson Phillip Albert	Basford, Isandula Road	Wicker Furn. Manuf	0	0			
Jackson Charles	Mansfield Woodhouse, New Mill Ln	Basket maker				0	
Janssens Emile	Newark	Basket maker				0	0
Kirk Ernest	Sherwood, Spondon Street	Basket maker				0	
Leivers Geo Henry	Bulwell, Highbury Vale	Basket maker	0	0		0	
Lord Roberts Workshops	Nottingham, Dame Agnes Street	Wicker Furn. Manuf		0			

A Basketful

20th Century Nottinghamshire basket makers sourced from Trade directories

Name	Address	BM detail	1908	1922	1936	1949	1957
Mallett Frdk Chas.	Basford, Park Lane	Wicker Chair Manuf			0		
Marshall Thomas	Sutton on Trent	Basket maker	0	0	0	0	
Mathieson Peter	Basford (Alexandra Works).	Basket maker	0	0	0		
Mills Horace	Newark, Farndon Road	Wicker Furn. Manuf	0	0		0	
Mills Mark William	East Leake	Wicker Furn. Manuf	0	0	0		
Mills Matthew & Son	East Leake	Wicker Furn. Manuf	0				
Morris, Wilkinson	Basford	Basket makers	0	0	0	0	
Newton Henry	Basford, Park Lane	Basket maker	0	0	0	0	
Noakes-Mooring C & Co	Mansfield, Pembroke Street	Basket maker			0	0	
Parberry & Buxton	Basford, Radford Road	Wicker Furn. Manuf				0	0
Patrick Richard	West Bridgford, Lady Bay Road	Basket maker	0				
Peacock Thomas	Southwell, Westgate	Basket maker				0	
Pearson Wm & Son	Basford, Gladstone Street	Wicker Furn. Manuf				0	
Pearson & Son Ltd	Nottingham, Angel Row	Basket makers	0	0			
Penney & Sons	Mansfield, Redcliffe Road	Basket maker	0	0			
Perkins Walter	Carrington, Loscoe Road	Basket maker	0				
Poetzing J	Basford, Duke Street	Wicker Furn. Manuf	0				
Rawson John Jnr	Elston	Basket maker	0	0			
Rice George	Barton in Fabis	Basket maker	0				
Richardson John	Bulwell, Robinson's Hill	Basket maker	0				
Rowland Albert	Hyson Green, Cornhill Street	Basket maker			0	0	0
Royal Nat. Inst. Blind	Nottingham, Chaucer Street	Basket makers	0	0	0	0	0
Savage George	Radford	Basket maker				0	
Sayers Bros & Co	Basford, Gladstone Street	Basket makers	0				
Scotney Mrs Eva	Mansfield, Queen Street	Basket maker			0		
Shaw Arthur & George	Basford, Westgate	Wicker Furn. Manuf	0				
Shaw Joseph	Basford, Radford Road	Basket maker			0		
Shaw Sam & Son	Basford, Queen Street	Wicker Chair Manuf			0		
Smith Clifford H	West Bridgford, Holme Road,	Basket maker				0	
Smith Miss Margaret	Nottingham, Sherwood Street	Basket maker	0				
Smith Willie	Nottingham, Carter Gate	Basket maker			0		
Smith & Peters	Nottingham, Granby Street	Basket makers				0	
Spencer Amos	Nottingham, Nottm Road	Wicker Chair Manuf			0		
Spencer Stephen	Basford, Percy Street	Wicker Furn. Manuf			0		
Stretton Herbert	Basford, Wilton Street	Wicker Furn. Manuf			0		
Summers Thomas Jnr	Sutton on Trent	Basket maker	0	0	0	0	0
Summers Thomas Snr	Sutton on Trent	BM & Rod Merchant	0				
Taylor George W	Basford, Wycliffe Street	Basket maker	0	0	0	0	
Taylor W James	Sutton on Trent	Basket maker	0	0			

20th Century Nottinghamshire basket makers sourced from Trade directories

Name	Address	BM detail	1908	1922	1936	1949	1957
Tomlinson Francis	Retford, Carolgate	Basket maker			0		
Tomlinson William	Nottingham, Chard Street	Wicker Furn. Manuf		0		0	
Truman Joseph	Basford, Bagnall Road	Wicker Furn. Manuf	0				
Walker John T	Basford, High Church Street	Wicker Furn. Manuf			0		
Watson John	Basford, Queen Street	Wicker Furn. Manuf	0				
White Charles	Nottingham, Western Street	Basket maker		0			
White Bros	Nottingham, Parliament Street	Basket maker	0	0	0	0	0
Whitehead A T	Nottingham, Ilkeston Road	Basket maker	0				
Willowbrook Co.	Basford, Jasmine Road	Wicker Furn. Manuf			0		
Winkler Hermann	Carrington, Jenner Street	Wicker Furn. Manuf	0				
Woods Albert Edwd	Sutton on Trent	Basket maker				0	0
Woods W	Sutton on Trent	Basket maker	0	0			
Woodward T & Son	Nottingham, Raleigh Street	Basket maker	0				
Wright Herbert	Hyson Green, Lenton Street	Wicker Furn. Manuf				0	0

Photograph of a group of unknown hamper workers in the Nottingham area c.1900.
Photo: picturethepast.

"Nottinghamshire is famed all over England for the curiosity of their workmanship in Wickerware"
- Charles Deering - History of Nottingham, 1751.

A Basketful

Basford basket makers 1861 - 1891, sourced from the Census

(Birth years are approximate)

Name	Address	Occ detail	Birthplace	Year	1861	1871	1881	1891
Adlington Thomas	Bagnall Rd	BM	Basford	1870				0
Allcock Thomas	Park Lane	BM	Farndon	1858			0	0
Angersbach Christian	High Street	BM * Empl.	Germany, Offenbach	1830	0	0	0	0
Atkinson Frederick	Nelson Street	BM	Basford	1858			0	
Atkinson William	Crooked Lane	BM	Basford	1858		0		
Attenborough Francis	Queen Square	BM appr	Basford	1880				0
Bailey Albert	Liddington St	BM appr	Derbys, Beighton?	1876				0
Ball Wm H	Westgate	BM	Bulwell	1874				0
Barker John	Bell Terrace	BM	Leics, Kegworth	1844			0	
Barks George	Church Place	BM	Basford	1858		0		
Barks Thomas	Nelson Street	BM	Basford	1856		0		
Barnes Charles	High Street	BM	Basford	1845	0	0		
Barnes Charles	High Street	BM	Basford	1844		0	0	0
Barnes Thos (son)	High Street	BM	Basford	1870				0
Barnes Alfred (son)	High Street	BM	Basford	1872				0
Barnes C Henry (son)	High Street	BM	Basford	1868				0
Barratt John	King Street	BM	Nottingham	1841		0		
Barsby Sml	Alice Square	Bm	Basford	1876				0
Barson Wm	Eland Street	BM appr	Derbys, Brampton	1873				0
Beecroft Ernest	North Gate	Peramb. Mkr	Basford	1877				0
Betteridge Geo	Zulu Road	BM appr	Derbys, Alfreton	1873				0
Bexon Arthur	David Lane	BM	Bulwell	1873				0
Bickerstaffe John	High St, Apple Row	BM	Basford	1870				0
Birchell Chas	Silverdale Road	BM	London	1864				0
Bird James	Wicklow Street	BM	Basford	1877				0
Birkett John	Ford Street	BM	Basford	1856		0	0	
Blatherwick Jos H	Springfield Street	BM	Derbys, Ilkeston	1868				0
Blee Harry	Springfield Street	Peramb. Manuf *Emp.	Cornwall, Penryn	1861				0
Blee Phillip	Mill Street	Peramb. Manuf	Cornwall, Penryn	1836			0	
Blunt Wm	Cowley Street	Wicker Furn Manuf	Northants, P'borough	1874				0
Bornber? Thos	Bailey Street	BM	Basford	1877				0
Bowley William	Queen Street	BM	Basford	1854		0		
Bracknell Herbert	Dob Alley	Willow Furn Maker	Bulwell	1866				0
Bradbury Elizabeth A	Church Street	Peramb. Trimmer	Hucknall	1854			0	
Bradbury Thomas	Church Street	Peramb. Asst	Linby	1819			0	
Brown Eliza Ann	Brown's Croft	BM	Basford	1856		0		
Brown George	High St, Jasons Row	BM	Basford	1875				0
Brown Reuben	Mount Pleasant	BM	Basford	1852		0	0	0
Brownlow Thomas	Queen Street	Peramb. Maker	Basford	1862			0	
Chambers Phillip	Liddington Street	BM	Nottm	1859	0			0
Chambers Thos	Radford Road	Basket Manuf * Emp.	Derbys, Sawley	1841			0	0
Chappell John	Vernon Road	BM	Rolleston	1867			0	
Chappell Joseph	Vernon Road	BM	Basford	1870				0
Chawmer Reuben	Church Street	BM	Basford	1868			0	

Basford basket makers 1861 - 1891, sourced from the Census
(Birth years are approximate)

Name	Address	Occ detail	Birthplace	Year	1861	1871	1881	1891
Cl......Wm J	Silverdale Road	BM	Long Sutton	1860				0
Clark Alfred	Osberton Street	BM * Empl.	Bulwell	1858				0
Clark Henry	Mosley Street	Bamboo Wkr	Herts, St Albans	1850				0
Clark Henry(son)	Mosley Street	BM	Northampton	1874				0
Clarke Ann	Park Lane	BM	Basford	1846	0			
Clarke Francis	Durnford Street	BM * Empl	Leics, Swithland	1843			0	0
Clarke George	Park Lane	BM	Basford	1847	0			
Clarke John	Browns Croft	BM	Basford	1874	0			
Clarke John	Westgate	BM	Basford	1841				0
Clarke Joseph	Park Lane	BM	Basford	1868			0	
Clarke Mary H (wife)	Browns Croft	BM upholsterer	Basford	1876				0
Cliffe Wm H	Ekowe Street	BM	Leics, Cas. Don.	1864				0
Constable Samuel	Lincoln Place	BM	Basford	1852		0	0	
Cox Geo. Wm.	Rose Yd, Mount Street	BM	Spalding	1878				0
Culley Chas E	Springfield Street	BM appr	Basford	1878				0
Cuttings Thos	Rawson Terr, Rope St	BM	Derbys, Chesterfield	1874				0
Cutts William	Dob Park	BM	Basford	1845	0			
Dabell Richard	High Street	BM	Bulwell	1876				0
Darwin? John	Aline Terr, John St	BM	Leics, Cas Don	1870				0
Dexter James	Queen Square	BM	Basford	1875				0
Diggle Ellen	Lincoln Street	BM	Basford	1854			0	
Diggle Nathan	High Street	BM	Lenton	1847		0		
Doncaster Wm	Radford Road	BM appr	Bulwell	1871				0
Drabble Thomas		BM	Basford	1859		0		
Eason Geo	Whitechapel Street	Osier Rod Peeler	Yorks, Castleford	1879				0
Fearn Alfred	Percy Street	BM	Basford	1854		0	0	
Foulds Ernest	Durnford Street	BM	Basford	1877				0
Fox Henry	Ekowe Street	BM	Leics, Thurmaston	1871				0
Frost Geo. Henry	Southwark Place	BM	Staffs, Burton on Trent	1855			0	
G__ler John	Browns Croft	BM	Basford	1869				0
Gamble Rebecca		BM	Basford	1853		0		
Green James	Queen Street	Peramb. Asst	York	1866			0	
Green John	Queen Street	Peramb. Maker	Radford	1839			0	
Green John A	Queen Street	Peramb. Asst	York	1868			0	
Greensmith Israel	Mill St, Albert Place	BM	Cinderhill	1864				0
Grocock Len/Lemuel	Westgate	Peramb. Manuf.	Basford	1856		0	0	
Hargeaves Thomas	Church Street	BM	Lancs, Blackburn	1817	0			
Hart Thomas		BM	Basford	1851		0		
Hearn Alfred	North Gate	BM *Empl.	Basford	1856				0
Henson John	Napoleon Square	BM	Basford	1878				0
Hickling Albert	Ekowe Street	BM	Worksop	1876				0
Hickling Mary Ann	Dob Park	BM	Basford	1843	0			
Hickman John	Waterford Street	BM	Staffs, Bloxwich	1877				0
Hind Geo	High Street	BM	Basford	1879				0

A Basketful

Basford basket makers 1861 - 1891, sourced from the Census

(Birth years are approximate)

Name	Address	Occ detail	Birthplace	Year	1861	1871	1881	1891
Hirst Margaret	Babworth Street	BM	Warw, Birmingham	1862				0
Hodson Joseph	Egypt Road	Art Wicker Furn Mkr	Farndon	1865				0
Holmes John	Whitemoor Road	BM	Bulwell	1870				0
Holroyd Jas	Whitemoor Road	BM	Sneinton	1853		0	0	0
Hooks Harry	Francis Gr. Vernon Ave	BM	Basford	1872				0
Housely Samuel	Westgate	Peramb. Manuf	Arnold	1831			0	
Humphries Florence	Wilton Street	BM assistant	Warw, Birmingham	1878				0
James ..... (female)	Dob Park	BM	Nottingham	1848	0			
King Thos	Browns Croft	BM	Nottingham	1874				0
Kingston Eliza	Queen Street	BM	Gloucs, Tewkesbury	1852		0		
Kingston Frederick	Nelson Street	BM	Basford	1858		0		
Kingston John	Queen Street	BM *Empl	Arnold	1835		0		
Kingston John	Alice Square	BM	Basford	1841			0	
Kingston John	Bulwell Lane	Peramb. Maker	Basford	1869				0
Kingston Samuel	Alice Square	Asst BM	Basford	1864			0	
Kingston Sml	Cheltenham St	BM	Gloucs. Tewkesbury	1849			0	0
Kinton John	High Street	BM appr	Warw. Coventry	1872				0
Kirk Christopher	Lincoln Street	BM & Grocer	Bulwell	1849		0		
Kirk Wm	Bailey Street	BM appr	Aslockton	1872				0
Kirk Wm	Bar Lane	BM	Basford	1876				0
Lanes James	Queen Street	BM	Basford	1817		0		
Latham Thomas	Queen's Square	BM	Warw. Birmingham	1849		0	0	
Leatherland Ben	Queen Street	BM	Basford	1859		0		
Leatherland John	Wycliffe Street	BM	Basford	1877				0
Leatherland Thos	Queen Street	BM	Basford	1857		0	0	0
Longden Thos.	Nottm Road	BM	Ches, Congleton	1850			0	0
Major?	Park Lane	Rod Splitter	Basford	1861		0		
Marsh Walter	Liddington Street	BM	Leicester	1870				0
Martin Thos	Crooked Lane	BM	Bulwell	1852		0		
Mason Walter	High Street	BM	Basford	1856		0		
Mason Wm	Arthur Terr, Palm St	Rod peeler & worker	Nottingham	1880				0
Mason Wm	Liddington Street	B Manuf * Empl.	Spalding	1847			0	0
Mason Wm H (son)	Liddington Street	BM	Grimsby	1872				0
Mather Albert	Monsall Street	BM	Basford	1878				0
Mathieson Peter	Eland Street	B & Furn Mkr *Empl	Denmark	1856				0
Meakin Samuel	Albert Place	BM	Basford	1853		0		
Meakin Thomas	Harker's Row	BM	Derbys, Staveley	1857		0	0	
Middleton William	Monsall Street	BM	Basford	1878				0
Mitchell William	Crooked Lane	BM	Basford	1854		0		
Morgan John	Queen Street	BM	Basford	1854		0		
Morley Mark	Whitemoor Road	BM	Basford	1872				0
Morley William	High Street	BM	Basford	1857		0		
Murphy John	Queen Street	BM	Basford	1836		0		
Newham John	Aline Terr, John St	Wicker Furn Mkr	Leics, Cas Don	1866				0

Basford basket makers 1861 - 1891, sourced from the Census
(Birth years are approximate)

Name	Address	Occ detail	Birthplace	Year	1861	1871	1881	1891
Newton Albert	Vernon Avenue	BM	Basford	1876				0
Newton Henry	Vernon Avenue	BM	Bulwell	1848		0	0	0
North Junia	Roberts Row	BM	Leics, Kegworth	1850				0
Paine Benj.	Chelsea Street	BM	Nottingham	1873				0
Pascoe Theodore	Mill Street	Peramb. Maker	Cornwall, Truro	1826		0	0	0
Penney Charles	Isandula Road	BM	Rutl, N. Luffenham	1831				0
Perkins Walter J	Adam's Place	BM	Nottingham	1846			0	0
Perkins Wm Jas	Mount Street	BM	Nottingham	1851				0
Perrons Noah	Lincoln Street	Peramb. Manuf.	Basford	1838		0		
Perrons Sarah	Tenter House Lane	BM	Basford	1841	0			
Perrons Thomas	Tinkerhouse Lane	BM	Basford	1862		0		
Pitcher Francis	Silverdale Road	BM	Norfolk, Sherbourne	1869				0
Rainbow Margaret	Park Lane	BM	Bulwell	1844		0		
Ranyard? Samuel	Park Lane	BM	Basford	1851		0		
Richardson James	Bailey Street	BM	Warw, Alcester	1876				0
Rick George	Park Lane	BM	Basford	1860		0		
Rickett John	Cheltenham Street	BM	Basford	1861			0	0
Samuel Arthur W	Zulu Road	BM appr	Cambr, Hauxton	1872				0
Sarson William	Springfield Street	BM	Leics, Thurmaston	1873				0
Sayers Christopher	Bailey Street	BM	Basford	1865				0
Saywood? Harriet	High Street	BM	Radford	1839	0			
Scaling William	Coal Pit Lane	BM Empl	Yorks, Hull	1820	0	0	0	
Scaling William	Mount Pleasant	BM *Empl	Basford	1866				0
Scott Fred	Wicklow Street	BM Salesman	Lancs, Manchester	1864				0
Scott Wm	Whitemoor Road	BM	Basford	1876				0
Seagrave Ernest	Chard Street	BM	Basford	1877				0
Self John	Ford Street	Osier peeler	Hucknall	1879				0
Shaw Harry	Cowley Street	BM	Basford	1876				0
Shaw John Henry	Whitemoor Road	BM	Basford	1877				0
Shaw Joseph	Whitemoor Road	BM	Basford	1855			0	0
Shaw Samuel	Queen Square	BM	Basford	1853			0	0
Shaw Samuel	Westgate	BM	Bulwell	1854			0	0
Shaw Wallace Albert	Whitemoor Road	BM	Basford	1875				0
Shaw Wm (son)	Queen Square	BM	Basford	1877				0
Sheffield Samuel	Lincoln Street	BM	Nottingham	1851		0		
Shimeld William	Liddington Street	BM	Staffs, Bottom Mdw	1872				0
Shipsides Albert J	Queen Street	BM	Derbys, Cromford	1854			0	
Shipsides Eliza (cau)	Browns Croft	BM	Basford	1878				0
Shipsides Jas	Browns Croft	BM	Basford	1854			0	0
Shipsides Thomas	Whitemoor Road	BM	Basford	1847		0		
Shipstone Thomas	Lincoln Street	BM	Basford	1835		0		
Sills William	Lincoln Terrace	Works @ BM	Basford	1857		0		
Smedley Samuel	Pryer? Street	BM	Derbys, Sawley	1874				0
Smith Catherine	Alice Sq, Queen St	Peramb. Trimmer	Chilwell	1860			0	

Basford basket makers 1861 - 1891, sourced from the Census

(Birth years are approximate)

Name	Address	Occ detail	Birthplace	Year	1861	1871	1881	1891
Spencer Ann	King Street	BM	Basford	1842		0		
Spencer Thos H	Bailey Street	Wicker Furn Maker	Basford	1871				0
Stevenson Edward	High Street	BM	Derbys, Breaston	1862		0		
Stevenson Samuel	High Street	BM	Derbys, Breaston	1856		0		
Stevenson William	Queen Street	BM	Radford	1876				0
Straw Samuel	Walker's Square	BM	Bulwell	1854			0	
Summers Walter	Amelia Yard	BM	Nottingham	1876				0
Summers Chas A.	Duke Street	BM	Basford	1877				0
Sunderland Albert	Springfield Street	BM	Yks, Huddersfield	1874				0
Sutton Thomas	Victoria Terrace	BM	Basford	1878				0
Tebbet William	North Street	BM	Basford	1856		0		
Thompson Thomas	Bulwell Lane	BM *Empl	Flintham	1844		0		
Thraves Albert	North Gate	Peramb. Mkr.	Basford	1856				0
Tilford John	Academy Place	BM	Basford	1855		0		
Torr William	High Street	BM	Basford	1863				0
Torr William	Terrace Drive	BM	Basford	1860			0	0
Towlson Thomas	Percy Street	BM	Basford	1870				0
Turner Francis	Liddington Street	BM	Derbys, Oakthorpe	1830				0
Tye Harriet		BM	Mansfield	1856		0		
Vickers Frank	Lincoln Street	BM	Beds, Oakley	1867			0	
Vickerstaff William	High Street	BM	Basford	1861			0	
Waterfield Mary Ann	Whitemoor Road	BM	Bulwell	1843	0			
Watson John	Queen Street	Peramb. Maker	Basford	1867			0	
Watson Thomas	Queen/Mill Street	BM	Basford	1856			0	0
White George	Westgate	BM	Basford	1856			0	
White John Rbt	Wilton Street	BM	Basford	1861			0	0
White William	Westgate	BM	Basford	1863			0	
Whitworth Walter	Whitemoor Road	BM	Basford	1873				0
Widdowson Chas	Radford Road	BM	Leics, Loughborough	1867				0
Widdowson Geo.H	Rawson Terr, Rope St	BM	Nottingham	1874				0
Widdowson Robert	King Street	BM	Leics, Loughborough	1840			0	
Widdowson Selina	Church Street	BM	Leics, Loughborough	1841			0	
Wildyard? Herbert	Prior Terrace	BM	Basford	1877				0
Wilkinson Herbert	High Street	BM	Basford	1875				0
Willman William	Hucknall Road	BM	Derbys, Measham	1813			0	0
Wright William	Bailey Street	BM *Empl	Bedford	1858			0	0

East and West Leake basket makers 1841 - 1901, sourced from the Census
(Birth years are approximate)

Name	Address	Occ detail	Birthplace	Year	1841	51	61	71	81	91	1901
Ayre Wm	EL Main Street	BM appr	Rempstone	1860					0	0	
Baxter Ellen	EL Carvers Yard	Osier Peeler	E. Leake	1873						0	
Belton Emma	EL West Street	Osier Peeler	E. Leake	1856							0
Blower Elizabeth	EL School Green	Osier Peeler	E. Leake	1846							0
Bolton Chas	EL Costock Rd	Wicker Chair Mkr	Northants, P'borough	1858							0
Bradbury Albert E	EL Main Street	BM appr	Surrey, Croydon	1874						0	
Bradbury Chas	EL Main Street	BM	Leics, Loughbor	1856						0	0
Bramley Frances J	EL School Green	Osier Peeler	E. Leake	1878						0	
Bramley Geo Henry	EL Main Street	BM appr	E. Leake	1875						0	
Bramley Jos. Ellis	EL Main Street	BM	E. Leake	1870						0	
Bramley Frank	EL Main Street	BM	E. Leake	1873						0	0
Burrows Thos	EL	BM	Derbys, Sawley	1856				0			
Burton Emerie	EL Normanton Rd	Wicker Worker	E. Leake	1874							0
Burton Emery	EL Brookside	BM	E. Leake	1852				0	0	0	
Burton Ernest	EL Main Street	BM	E. Leake	1860						0	
Burton Ernie	EL Main Street	BM	E. Leake	1872						0	
Carver Henry	EL The Green	BM	E. Leake	1852				0			
Clarke Wm	EL Costock Rd	BM appr	E. Leake	1858				0	0	0	
Colorm? Chas Wm	EL Pleasant Rise	BM	E. Leake	1861						0	
Crowson Wm	EL Main Street	BM appr	E. Leake	1876						0	
Crump Rd Chas	EL Loughbor Rd	BM	Worcs, Stourbridge	1873						0	
Doughty Richard	EL The Stocks	BM	E. Leake	1870						0	0
Duffty Ernest	EL Main Street	BM	E. Leake	1876						0	0
Dutton John	EL	BM appr	Gotham	1845			0				
Fromman? John	EL	BM	Leics, Prestwold	1851				0			
Garner James	EL East Street	BM appr	E. Leake	1858			0	0			
Godber Geo	EL Costock Rd	BM	Leics, Loughbor	1882							0
Godber John Hugh	EL Main Street	BM	Leics, Loughbor	1854						0	0
Godber John Thos.	EL Main Street	BM appr	Leics, Loughbor	1874						0	0
Godber William	EL Main Street	BM appr	Leics, Loughbor	1876						0	
Goodacre Horace	EL The Green	BM	E. Leake	1855						0	
Gunn Thos	EL West St, Mills Yd	BM	E. Leake	1850					0	0	0
Gunn J. Haywood	EL Main Street	BM appr	E. Leake	1875						0	
Gunn Thos	EL East Street	BM	E. Leake	1883							0
Hallam Arthur	EL Castle	BM appr	E. Leake	1859					0		
Hallam Edward	EL Castle	BM appr	E. Leake	1858					0	0	
Hallam Ernest Jos	EL Main Street	BM	E. Leake	1872						0	

A Basketful

East and West Leake basket makers 1841 - 1901, sourced from the Census

(Birth years are approximate)

Name	Address	Occ detail	Birthplace	Year	1841	51	61	71	81	91	1901
Hallam Harry	EL Castle Hill	BM appr	E. Leake	1876						0	
Hallam Herbert	EL Loughbor Rd	BM	E. Leake	1869						0	0
Hallam Jas Arthur	EL Castle Hill	BM	E. Leake	1870						0	0
Hallam John H	EL Chapel Yard	BM appr	E. Leake	1875							0
Hallam Wm	EL Castle Hill	BM	E. Leake	1881							0
Haywood Emma	EL West Sreet	Osier Peeler	Leics, Quorn	1842							0
Haywood Thos	EL Main Street	BM	E. Leake	1850						0	
Henson Wm	EL Chapel Yard	BM appr	E. Leake	1875						0	0
Holland Francis	EL Gotham Rd	Journeyman BM	Costock	1826		0	0				
Holland Francis	EL	Journeyman BM	Costock	1846				0			
Howitt William	EL Loughbor Rd	BM	Staffs, Burton on T	1834						0	0
Jackson Henry	EL Long Row	BM	Scotland	1856							0
Levi Henry John	EL East Street	BM	Nottingham	1839				0			
Marshall Walter	EL The Nook	BM	E. Leake	1869						0	0
Marshall Henry/Harry	EL Main Street	BM	E. Leake	1865						0	0
Millington Wm	EL Main Street	BM appr	Costock	1861					0		0
Mills Albert	EL Mills Yard	BM	E. Leake	1868					0		
Mills Albert Edwd	EL Main Street	BM	E. Leake	1865					0		
Mills Alfred	WL	BM	W. Leake	1819		0		0	0	0	
Mills Arthur	WL	Asst BM	W. Leake	1877						0	
Mills Augustus	EL Costock Rd	Wicker Chair Mkr	E. Leake	1874							0
Mills Dick	WL	BM	W. Leake	1857					0		
Mills Edward	Sutton Bonington	BM	Sutton Bonington	1856					0	0	0
Mills Edward	Sutton Bonington	BM	W. Leake	1815		0	0	0	0		
Mills Emma	EL The Green	BM empl 6m3b	Cambs, Outwell	1841				0			
Mills Felix Wm	EL Mills Yard	B Manuf	Derbys, Mapperley	1863						0	
Mills Frederick	EL Main Street	BM	E. Leake	1860						0	0
Mills Fredk Saml	EL Mills Yard	BM	E. Leake	1863					0		
Mills Gautwood E	EL West Street	Osier Peeler	E. Leake	1883							0
Mills George	EL The Green	B Manuf	E. Leake	1843			0				
Mills George	EL Main Street	BM Skein	E. Leake	1871						0	0
Mills John	EL Pinfold Grn	BM	W. Leake	1799	0	0					
Mills John	EL Pinfold Grn	BM *Empl	E. Leake	1829		0	0		0		
Mills John H	EL Main Street	BM	E. Leake	1866					0		
Mills John Horace	EL Mills Yard	BM	E. Leake	1857					0	0	
Mills Joseph	WL	BM	W. Leake	1810	0	0		0			
Mills Joshua (son)	EL Pinfold Grn	BM	E. Leake	1837		0	0	0			

East and West Leake basket makers 1841 - 1901, sourced from the Census
(Birth years are approximate)

Name	Address	Occ detail	Birthplace	Year	1841	51	61	71	81	91	1901
Mills Luke	WL	BM	W. Leake	1836			0				
Mills Mark Wm	EL Main Street	Skein BM *Empl	E. Leake	1838					0	0	0
Mills Mary	EL The Green	B Manuf	Wysall	1802			0				
Mills Matthew (son)	WL	BM	W. Leake	1831		0	0			0	0
Mills Oliver	WL	BM	W. Leake	1825			0				
Mills Thos	EL West Street	BM	E. Leake	1811			0	0			
Mills Walter	EL Mills Yard	B Manuf	W. Leake	1831						0	
Mills Walter Harry	EL Main Street	Skein BM	E. Leake	1866					0	0	0
Mills William	EL Gotham Rd	BM	W. Leake	1802		0	0	0			
Mills William	WL	BM & Victualler	W. Leake	1775	0	0					
Mills Wm	WL Main Street	BM	W. Leake	1855				0	0	0	0
Mills Wm	EL The Castle	BM	Sutton Bonington	1841			0	0	0		
Mott David	EL Costock Rd	BM appr	Norfolk, Markham	1874						0	
Needham Thos.	EL School Green	BM	Costock	1871							0
Osborne Arthur	EL Carvers Yd	BM	E. Leake	1873						0	
Osborne Chas W	EL Costock Rd	BM	E. Leake	1861							0
Osborne Wm	EL Costock Rd	BM	E. Leake	1861					0		
Pepper Percy W	EL Back Yard	BM appr	E. Leake	1885							0
Pick Alice	EL School Green	Osier Peeler	E. Leake	1880							0
Pick Ada	EL School Green	Osier Peeler	E. Leake	1884							0
Pierpoint Ernest	EL Pleasant Rise	BM appr	E. Leake	1877						0	
Poundrill Arthur	EL Main Street	BM appr	Costock	1875						0	0
Roulstone Albert	EL Mills Yard	Skein BM	Radcliffe on Trent	1841					0		0
Roulstone David	EL East St, Bk Yd	BM	Radcliffe on Trent	1850				0			
Roulstone Fredk	EL Costock Rd	BM	Leics, Cas Don	1867					0		
Roulstone Geo	EL East St, Bk Yd	BM	Radcliffe on Trent	1829				0			
Roulstone Harriet	EL Main Street	Osier Peeler	E. Leake	1856						0	0
Roulstone John A	EL Carvers Yard	BM appr	E. Leake	1884							0
Roulstone Saml	EL West Street	Skein BM	Radcliffe on Trent	1841				0			
Roulstone Thomas	EL Costock Rd	BM	Radcliffe on Trent	1853					0	0	0	0
Roulstone Wm	EL New Road	BM	Radcliffe on Trent	1856					0	0	0	0
Sanders Wm	EL Castle Hill	BM	E. Leake	1879						0	0
Savage Clifton	EL Main Street	BM appr	E. Leake	1873						0	0
Savage Harry	EL Normanton Rd	Wicker work appr	E. Leake	1886							0
Savage Thos	EL The Green	BM	E. Leake	1870						0	0
Shepherd Chas	EL The Green	BM (deaf)	Stanford on Soar	1852						0	0
Shepherd Chas	EL Roadside	Skein BM	Sutton Bonington	1854					0		

East and West Leake basket makers 1841 - 1901, sourced from the Census

(Birth years are approximate)

Name	Address	Occ detail	Birthplace	Year	1841	51	61	71	81	91	1901
Smith Albert	EL The Green	BM appr	E. Leake	1877						0	0
Smith John	EL Roadside	Skein BM	Leics, Kegworth	1852						0	0
Smith Martha (wife)	EL East Street	Osier Peeler	E. Leake	1879							0
Statham Jas	EL Loughbor Rd	BM	Leics, Ashby' Zouch	1865						0	0
Taylor Edward	EL Costock Rd	BM	E. Leake	1859						0	0
Taylor Fred	EL Chapel Yd	BM	E. Leake	1881							0
Tomlinson Geo	EL	Skein BM	Leics, Cas Don	1850			0	0			
Tromman John	EL East Street	BM	Leics, Prestwold	1851				0			
Wells Wm	EL	BM	Leics, Cas Don	1848				0	0		
Whitby Arthur	EL Main Street	BM	E. Leake	1871						0	0
Whitby Fred	EL Main Street	BM	E. Leake	1873						0	
Whitby Jane	EL Main Street	Osier Peeler	E. Leake	1875						0	
Whitby John	EL Main Street	BM	E. Leake	1870						0	0
White William	EL Workhouse. Yd	BM	E. Leake	1872						0	
Winks George	EL Castle Hill	BM	Hyson Green	1874							0

An excellent and comprehensive study project by East Leake & District Local History publication, '200 years of basket making in Ratcliffe on Soar, West Leake and East Leake, Nottinghamshire'. The book covers in some detail, the families, workers, workshops and the Mills family tree. It is a recommended read and source of reference to all those interested in basketry and these villages.

More lovely examples of willow and rush from the East Leake workshops, c.1900

86 A Basketful

Sutton on Trent basket makers 1861 - 1901, sourced from the Census
(Birth years are approximate)

Name	Birthplace	Year	Occupation	1861	1871	1881	1891	1901
Bailey James	Mddx, Spittalfield	1822	Basket maker			0		
Bird Alfred	Sutton on Trent	1871	Basket maker				0	0
Brandon Peter	USA, Pittsburgh	1835	Basket maker		0	0	0	
Chapman William	Lincoln	1801	Basket maker	0				
Clark Francis	Leics, Swithland	1843	Basket maker					0
Clark William	Sutton on Trent	1885	BM Appr					0
Cob Ellen	Sutton on Trent	1856	Rod Peeler				0	
Cobb Catherine	Sutton on Trent	1852	Rod Peeler & Sorter					0
Doughty Robert	Yorks, Hull	1847	Basket maker		0	0	0	0
Freeman Arthur	Sutton on Trent	1870	Willow Merchant					0
Freeman David	East Markham	1838	Willow Merchant					0
Freeman William	Newton on Trent	1865	Basket maker				0	0
Hall James Richard	Papplewick	1870	Basket maker				0	
Hallam Ann	Bardney	1846	Rod Peeler					0
Handley Arthur	Sutton on Trent	1876	Basket maker appr				0	
Hardy Elizabeth	Yorks, Hull	1846	Basket maker			0		
Hardy Thomas	Yorks, Hull	1847	Basket maker			0		
Hayes Hannah	Sutton on Trent	1882	Rod Peeler & Sorter					0
Hayes Harriet	Balderton	1834	Rod Peeler & Sorter					0
Haywood Elijah	Hants, Portsea	1840	Basket maker			0		
Haywood Henry	Sutton on Trent	1876	Basket maker appr				0	
Haywood Herbert	Sutton on Trent	1878	Basket maker appr				0	
Heys William	Lancs, Mawdesley	1840	Basket maker			0		
Hinchcliffe Joseph	Sutton on Trent	1868	Basket maker				0	
Hinchcliffe Caroline	Langford	1851	Rod Peeler					0
Holmes Walter	Sutton on Trent	1877	Basket maker appr				0	
Hunt Sarah	Sutton on Trent	1879	Rod Peeler					0
Mackender Henry	Staunton	1877	Basket maker appr				0	
Maples Robert	Sutton on Trent	1843	Basket maker			0	0	
Marsden Peter	Lancs, Mawdesley	1842	Basket maker			0		
Marshall Francis E	Sutton on Trent	1887	Basket maker appr					0
Marshall Thomas	Sutton on Trent	1860	Basket maker			0	0	0	0
Marshall John	Sutton on Trent	1823	Master B. Mkr		0	0	0	
McDonald George	Lancs, Manchester	1857	Basket maker appr		0			
McDonald William	Ireland	1841	Basket maker		0	0		
Mumford George	Devon, Plymouth	1856	Basket maker				0	0	0
Nichols John	Norfolk, E. Runton	1841	Basket maker		0			
Parkin Arthur	Sutton on Trent	1869	Basket maker				0	
Parkins William	Leics, Loughborough	1809	Basket maker				0	
Parkins Elizabeth	Newark	1805	Basket maker				0	

A Basketful

Sutton on Trent basket makers 1861 - 1901, sourced from the Census
(Birth years are approximate)

Name	Birthplace	Year	Occupation	1861	1871	1881	1891	1901
Phillips John	Boston	1806	Basket maker	0				
Pierrepont William	Sutton on Trent	1873	Basket maker's Lab				0	
Plumb Ada	Burton Joyce	1882	Rod Peeler					0
Richards Thomas	Sutton on Trent	1856	Basket maker			0	0	0
Richardson Edwin	Lancs, Manchester	1839	Basket maker	0				
Ricvhardson Emma	Lancs, Manchester	1838	Basket maker	0				
Saunderson John	Cromwell	1815	Basket labourer	0				
Shipley Edric	Sutton on Trent	1883	Basket maker					0
Shipley Edwin	Sutton on Trent	1874	Journeyman B. Maker				0	0
Shipley Elizabeth	Sutton on Trent	1849	Rod Peeler					0
Shipley John	Sutton on Trent	1881	Basket maker					0
Simcox George	London	1843	Basket maker	0				
Stephens George	Gloucs,Tewkesbury	1830	Packer	0				
Summers Fanny	Newark	1843	Empl. Basket making				0	
Summers Henry	Newark	1847	Basket maker	0				
Summers Joseph	Sutton on Trent	1875	Basket maker				0	
Summers Thomas	Newark	1845	Basket maker	0	0	0		0
Summers Thomas	Sutton on Trent	1872	Basket maker				0	0
Summers Lizzie	Sutton on Trent	1871	Empl. Basket making				0	
Taylor Geo Henry	Lancs. Southport	1862	Basket maker			0	0	0
Taylor William	Sutton on Trent	1878	Basket maker				0	0
Taylor William J	Lancs, Southport	1864	Basket maker			0	0	0
Taylor William	Lancs, Mawdesley	1834	Basket maker		0	0	0	0
Thorpe Ann	Sutton on Trent	1839	Rod Peeler	0				
Trevor Emma	Marnham	1838	Basket maker				0	
Trevor Henry	Louth	1832	Basket maker				0	
Turner Sarah	Sutton on Trent	1865	Rod Peeler					0
Wallhead William	Sutton on Trent	1873	Basket maker				0	
Warn Edwin	London	1851	Basket maker					0
Wass Joseph	Leicester	1816	Basket maker	0				
Welch William	Lancs, Mawdesley	1841	Basket maker	0	0			
Whittington Thomas	Derby	1842	Basket maker			0	0	0
Willis Catherine	Sutton on Trent	1852	Rod Peeler	0				
Willis George.	Sutton on Trent	1849	Varnisher & Finisher	0				
Wood Mary Ann	Northampton	1844	Basket maker	0				
Wood William	Herts, Royston,	1843	Basket maker	0			0	0
Woods Albert Edwd	Sutton on Trent	1872	Basket maker				0	0
Woods Charles Fred	Sutton on Trent	1874	Basket maker				0	0
Woods William	Northampton	1870	Basket maker				0	
York Rebecca	Keyworth	1884	Rod Peeler					0

Southwell - Mills workers sourced from the 1891 Census
(Ages are approximate)

Name	Address	Age	Birthplace	Basket making detail
Atkinson George	Back Lane	36	Basford	Basket maker
Bell Emma	Kirklington Road	24	Farndon	Rod Peeler
Bell George	Westgate	30	Southwell	Basket maker
Bell John	Westgate	22	Southwell	empl @ Basket Wks
Bell Mary E	Westgate	21	Southwell	empl @ Basket Wks
Brake Martin	Easthorpe, Cottam Yd	13	Dorset, Lyme Regis	Basket maker's appr
Capson Samuel	Westgate	37	Nottingham	Basket maker
Dixon John W	Easthorpe	20	Farndon	Basket maker
Dixon Mary	Kirklington Road	39	Farndon	Rod Peeler
Dixon George	Kirklington Road	13	Farnsfield	Rod Peeler
Foster George W	Westhorpe	18	Southwell	Basket maker's appr
Foster George	King Street	22	London, Bermondsey	Basket maker
Gasgoigne John	Kirklington Road	24	Southwell	Rod Merchant's labourer
Gasgoigne William	Kirklington Road	22	Southwell	Basket maker
Hazlewood Robert	Easthorpe, Cottam Yd	29	Yorks, Selby	Basket maker
Hickinbottom Thomas	King Street	29	Castle Donington	Basket maker
Hind Samuel	King Street	16	Mansfield	Rod Buffer
Hudson William	King Street	29	Derby	Rod Buffer
Jepson Eliza	Westgate	13	Southwell	Rod Buffer
Jepson Emma	Westgate	15	Southwell	Rod Buffer
Longbottom Frank	Easthorpe	15	Farndon	Basket maker's appr
Longbottom Joseph	Easthorpe	17	Farndon	Basket maker
Marshall John	Court Ho, Burgage	17	Gringley on the Hill	Basket maker
Measham Richard	Kirklington Road	52	Derbys, Repton	Basket maker
Measham William	Kirklington Road	19	Leics, Ashby de la Zouch	Basket maker
Mills Augustus	Westgate	17	East Leake	Basket maker
Mills John H	Kirklington Road	34	East Leake	Willow Merchant
Mills Marion	Kirklington Road	31	London, Wandsworth	Wife of John Horace
Mills (children)	Kirklington Road		Southwell	William E 2, Florence 1yr
Mills (children)	Kirklington Road		Southwell	Edith 6 yrs, Horace A 4yrs.
Moore Harry	Back Lane	16	Southwell	Basket maker's appr
Noakes William	Kirklington Road	29	London, Wandsworth	Basket Mkr (Manager)
Peacock Thomas	Normanton	21	Hunts, Kimbolton	Basket maker
Stanley Edward	Westgate	15	Yorks, Brotton	Rod Buffer
Stanley Frederick	Westgate	19	Yorks, Saltburn	Rod Buffer
Stevenson Agnes	Back Lane	28	Southwell	Rod Peeler
Stevenson George	Easthorpe	36	Farndon	Buff Rod Peeler
Stevenson John	Back Lane	28	Farndon	Rod Peeler
Thornelly William	Kirklington Road	14	Southwell	Basket maker's appr.
Wells Mary	Back Lane	35	Southwell	Rod Peeler
Wood Henry	Back Lane	19	Southwell	Basket maker

A Basketful

Willow Timeline through Nottinghamshire and Lincolnshire

1616   Gainsborough – Robert Bowlston, alias Hubbard, basket maker, probate inventory (LA)

1651   Apprenticeship agreement – Thos. Byron of Lincoln and Thos. Tabor of Farndon (LA)

1663   Carlton on Trent – Stephen Smeeton, skep maker with 3 acre willow holt (NA)

1697   Oxton- reference to skein basket maker (NA)

1710   Harrison's business founded according to letterhead

1723   Harlaxton – Mathew Hutchinson, basket maker, bond reference (LA)

1731   Collingham – John Eyre, poor child of the parish, indenture to basket maker (NA)

1735   Stamford – John Lion 13 years old apprenticed to John Lyon, basket maker (LA)

1740   Bulcote – Isaac Dixon, basket maker, inventory (NA)

1742   West Leake – Osier bed owned by Mills family

1745   East Stoke –William Gee listed as scuttle maker – Parish Register (NA)

1767   Sleaford – William Ellmore listed as basket maker

1790   Lincoln – John Baxter, John and William Curtois listed as basket makers – Directory

1790   Newark – 10 basket makers listed in Trade Directory

1800   Stamford – Geo. Ratcliffe basket maker. Basket making family until 1950s

1822   Lincolnshire – 22 basket makers listed in Trade Directory

1824   Nottinghamshire – 73 Willow holts marked on 1st Edition O.S. Maps

1826   Lincolnshire – 35 basket makers listed in Pigot's Directory

1830   Barrow on Humber – William Barrick listed as basket maker.

1835   Grantham – Samuel Harrison, listed as basket maker in Walkergate – Pigot's Directory

1861   Basford – William Scaling, willow grower employing 27 men, 26 boys and 27 girls

1867   Sutton on Trent – 'Buffing' discovery by John Marshall

1871   Sutton on Trent – 27 basket makers listed in village, only 9 born locally

1871   Lincolnshire – 44 basket makers listed in County – not including seasonal or part time workers.

1881   Grantham –WB Harrison employs 40 men, 14 boys, 19 women – one of largest employers in UK

1881   Nottinghamshire 245 basket makers, Lincolnshire 281(excl. seasonal workers), UK - 7,000

1891   Nottinghamshire nearly 500 basket makers – Lincolnshire over 320 (excl. seasonal workers)

1895   Newark – Mills factory employs over 300

1900   Basford – Morris Wilkinson employs 400 workers. Approx 1,000 within the 'Basford triangle'

1917   Nottinghamshire – 500 acres of willows under cultivation

1921   Lincolnshire – 472 basket makers in county – (73 Grantham, 24 Grimsby/Cleethorpes) – Census

1956   East Leake – last basket making workshop closes, Chris Mills at the Beehive Works

c.1964   Newark and Grantham – last basket making factories close. (Mills and Harrison)

Key: LA – Lincolnshire Archives and NA – Nottinghamshire Archives

Bibliography – willow growing and basket making

BAGSHAWE T.W., *Basket making in Bedfordshire,* Luton Museum, 1981.

BASHAM Andrew, *How to make Hurdles from Willow.*

BASKET & CANE TRADES & WILLOW GROWERS JOURNAL, 1928

BOBART H.H., *Basketry through the ages,* 1936

BOBART H.H., *Records of the Basket maker's Company,* 1911

BROWN Tony, *WB Harrison & Sons and their Workforce.* Typescript, 2003

EAST LEAKE & Dist Local History Society, *200 years of Basket making,* 2001

ELLMORE Wm Palgrave, *The Cultivation of Osiers and Willows,* 1919

FITZRANDOLPH H.E. and HAY M.D., *Osier growing and Basketry,* 1926

GABRIEL S. & GOYMER S., *Complete Book of basketry Techniques,* 1991

HESELTINE Alastair, *Baskets and Basketmaking,* Shire Publications, 1986

HUTCHINSON H.P., *Willow growing and Basketmaking as Rural Industries,* 1916

INDUSTRIAL NOTTINGHAM, *Basket making in Nottingham,* article, Vol 30 No 6, 1950

JENKINS J. Geraint, *Traditional Country Craftsmen,* RKP Publications, 1965

KNOCK A.J., *Willow basket Work,* Dryad Press, 1979

LEGG Evelyn, *Country Baskets,* Mills & Boon, 1960

NEWHOLME Christopher, *Willows – the Genus Salix,* 1992

NOTTINGHAM GUARDIAN, *Annual Trade Review* 1924, features local Basket Making firms.

OKEY Thomas, *The Art of basket making,* 1912

OKEY Thomas, *A Basketful of Memories,* Dent 1930.

OSIERS and Willows, Ministry of Agriculture, Bulletin 89, 1913.

ORDNANCE SURVEY, *Maps,* 1st edition reprint, David & Charles.

PACKAGING – British Standards Institute, 1964

PHILLIPS Corinne E., *Skeps and Scuttles, Notts 17th C – to 1939,* Dissertation, Univ of Nottingham

SCALING William, *The Salix or Willow,* series of papers, 1871/2, (Nottingham Library)

STAMP Dudley, *Land Utilisation Survey part 60, Nottinghamshire,* 1944

STOTT K.G., *Cultivation and Use of Basket Willow,* Basketmaker's Association, 2001

VICTORIA COUNTY HISTORY, *Willow growing & basket making from 1750,* Notts Vol 1 & 2.

WARNES Jon, *Living Willow Sculpture,* Search Press, 2000.

WRIGHT Dorothy, *Complete Book of Baskets and Basketry,* 1977

Basket making terms

BASSINET / BASSINETTE - a type of cradle, often with openwork to the sides.

BUFFING – a process to stain the rod by using the natural dye in the willow skin, enhanced by boiling, then stripped/peeled to reveal the colour. This process was discovered by the Marshall family of Sutton on Trent, c.1868.

BOLT – bundle of willows, tied with willow rod. Bolt sold by weight.

BUTT – thick end of the willow rod.

CREEL – originally a Scottish term for a basket, today used to describe a type of angling basket.

FEDGE – a combined fence/hedge.

FITCHING – openwork, leaving the stakes/uprights as the main framework i.e. minimal weaving.

FLASKET – a shallow basket.

HAMPER – large rectangular basket, with cover/lid, often for factory storage/transit. Also formerly used in laundries, theatres and post offices.

HOLT – the area of land in which willows are cultivated. An osier or withy bed is an alternative term.

MAUND – a tall straight sided basket often for fish or potatoes.

NEST – set of usually three baskets, designed to fit inside each other for transit.

OSIER - another name of French origin for willow, (though strictly Salix viminalis).

PANNIER – basket designed to be carried by a horse or similar. Often used as a container to take dairy products to market. Also term used for baskets for airborne supplies and drops.

PLANK – low sloping platform - the basket maker's work surface.

PUNNET - basket of veneer strips, usually oak. Once a popular container for strawberries.

RAND – weave using a single rod in front, then behind the upright stakes. Most common weave.

ROD BRAKE/PEELER – hand-tool for removing the skin/bark of the willow.

RODS – the individual willows, depending on variety from 1m to 4m in length. (see also withy).

SCUTTLE – shallow form of heavy duty basket.

SEEDLIP - basket carried over the shoulder and used for sowing/broadcasting seed in the field.

SKEIN - willow rod split into three or four sections, then used for weaving fine basketry.

SKEP - heavy duty basket formerly used locally for carrying coal, gypsum etc.

SLEWING – weaving two or more rods in and out of the upright stakes.

TIP – thin end of the individual rod.

TWIGGY – term used to describe willow workers in Nottinghamshire (particularly Basford).

UPSETT – setting up the sides/uprights and linking to the base.

WICKER – a basketry product.

WITHY – a term used in SW England to describe the willow rod.

Placename Index

Place	Pages
Alford	53-55, 61, 63, 65
Algarkirk	59
Arnold	70, 75, 80
Aslockton	71, 80
Balderton	22, 38, 71, 87
Bardney	60, 87
Barrow on Humber	5, 53, 56, 57, 61, 62, 90
Barrowby	30
Barton in Fabis	42, 66, 70-72, 76
Barton on Humber	56
Basford	4, 6, 9, 11, 22, 31, 46-49, 60, 61, 68, 70, 73, 75-82, 89-90
Bassingham	5, 6, 19, 22, 68
Beckingham (Notts)	4-6, 22, 24, 75, 97
Bedfordshire	82, 91
Belgium	9, 43
Bilborough	71
Bingham	6, 22, 67-69, 72, 73
Bleasby (Notts)	4
Blyth	5, 22, 41, 66, 73, 75
Bole	5, 13, 22
Bonby	56
Boston	5, 37, 53-55, 57-63, 68
Boughton (Notts)	68
Bourne	31, 55, 56, 58, 60, 62, 63
Brant Broughton	63, 64
Brigg	53, 55, 57, 59, 61, 63
Bristol	69
Brocklesby	6
Brough (Notts)	57
Broughton	57, 61
Buckinghamshire	74
Bulcote	90
Bulwell	68, 69, 71-76, 78-82
Burton Coggles	57
Burton Joyce	18, 88
Calverton	18
Cambridgeshire	22, 58, 61, 74, 81, 84
Canada	44
Carlton Netherfield	66
Carlton on Trent	6, 16, 22, 90
Carlton Scroop	60
Carrington	48, 76, 77
Caunton	12
Cheshire	80
Chilwell	22, 61, 74 ,81
Cinderhill	69, 79
Clarborough	5, 70, 71
Claypole	38
Clee	57, 58, 60
Cleethorpes	5, 57, 58, 90
Collingham	16, 68, 70, 72-73, 90
Colwick	9, 22
Cornwall	78, 81
Costock	70, 84, 85
Cottam	4, 22, 73, 97
Cowbit	6, 13, 19
Cromwell	6, 22, 67, 69-72, 88
Crowland	5, 54, 56, 58, 60, 62
Crowle	54
Daybrook	75
Deeping St James	53, 55, 57, 59
Denmark	47, 80
Derbyshire	68, 70, 71, 73, 78-84, 88, 89.
Devon	58
Donington (Lincs)	53
Dorset	68, 89
Dry Doddington	20, 31, 38
Dunham	22, 69, 97
Dunston	60
East Leake	6, 8, 12, 22, 38-9, 46, 50-52, 66, 71, 76, 83-86, 90-91
East Markham	5, 87
East Stoke	5, 22, 41, 58, 66-70, 72, 74, 90
Elston	5, 12, 42, 68, 72, 74, 76
Epworth	53
Essex	57
Farndon	4, 5, 12, 22, 38, 40, 68-71, 73, 74, 78, 80, 89-90, 97
Farnsfield	69, 89
Fiskerton (Notts)	18, 22, 38
Flintham	74, 82
France	9, 15
Gainsborough	4, 5, 22-23, 29, 53-55, 57-63, 71, 90
Gedling	66

Placename Index

Place	Pages
Germany	59, 78
Gloucestershire	80, 88
Gonalston	22
Gotham	83
Goxhill	5
Grantham	4-6, 20, 30-36, 54-63, 72, 74, 90
Great Gonerby	59, 63
Grimsby	6, 54, 56-63, 65, 80, 90
Gringley	60, 71, 89
Gunthorpe (Notts)	68, 71
Hampshire	56, 87
Hardwick (Lincs)	5
Harlaxton	90
Hayton	5
Heckington	63
Hertfordshire	79, 88
Hickling	69
Hogsthorpe	61, 62
Holbeach	54, 55, 61, 63
Horncastle	30, 53-57, 59-60, 62, 69
Hucknall	78, 81
Huntingdonshire	72, 73, 89
Hyson Green	66, 76, 77, 86
Ingham	61
Ireland	16, 57, 58, 87
Keelby	57
Kelstern	59
Keyworth	88
Kimberley	71
Kirkstead	69
Kirton (Boston)	61
Kirton Lindsey	59, 63
Laceby	57
Lancashire	5, 16, 45, 56, 58, 69-70, 73, 74, 79, 81, 87-88,
Laneham	5
Langford	87
Laxton	6
Leicestershire	3-5, 11, 30, 46, 56, 58, 61, 68, 70-74, 78-89,
Lenton (Notts)	5, 68, 70, 72, 74, 79.

Place	Pages
Linby	70, 78
Lincoln	6, 16, 19, 26, 53-63, 68-69, 73, 87, 90
London	16, 29, 56, 58, 69, 71, 73, 78, 88-89
Long Sutton	53, 54, 60, 62, 79
Lound	4, 6, 22
Louth	53-59, 61-63, 73, 88
Lowdham	68, 69, 72, 75
Mansfield	66, 68-70, 73, 76, 82, 89
Mansfield W/house	75
Manthorpe	58-61
Market Deeping	55, 61
Market Rasen	6, 54, 56, 61-63
Marnham	88
Marton (Lincs)	73
Mattersey	70
Messingham	60
Metheringham	55, 60-62
Middlesex	56, 87
Milton	5
Miningsby	57
Morton (Notts)	38
Muskham	72, 74, 97
Netherlands	9
Newark	5-6, 14, 18, 21, 25-26, 28, 30, 38-40, 43-44, 56, 66-76, 87, 88, 90
Newton on Trent	5, 87
Norfolk	58, 60, 69, 71, 81, 85, 87
Normanton (Lincs)	31
Normanton on Trent	16
North Cotes	6
North Leverton	22
North Somercotes	60
North Wheatley	5
Northamptonshire	56-57, 59-60, 68, 71-74, 78-79, 83, 88
Northumberland	60, 73
Norwell	6, 12, 22, 30, 61, 70, 74
Nottingham	5-6, 28-29, 31, 37-38, 66-78, 80-82, 84, 89, 91

94   *A Basketful*

Placename Index

Place	Pages
Ordsall	68, 74
Owston Ferry	54, 58-59, 62, 65
Oxfordshire	69
Oxton	90
Papplewick	87
Plumtree	68
Poland	45
Prussia	9
Radcliffe on Trent	46, 67, 71, 73, 85
Radford	11, 58, 66, 70-72, 74-76, 79, 81-82
Rampton	22
Ratcliffe on Soar	67, 86
Redmile	72
Rempstone	83
Retford	5, 22, 29, 41, 66-74, 77
Rolleston	6, 22, 78
Rufford (Notts)	73
Rutland	58-60, 72, 81
Saxilby	25, 37
Saxondale	68
Scamblesby	57
Scopwick	59
Scotland	9, 38, 60, 84
Scotton	59
Scunthorpe	62
Shelford	22. 68, 71
Sherwood	67, 72, 75
Sibthorpe	42
Silk Willoughby	56
Skegness	37
Sleaford	30-31, 53-55, 57, 59, 62-63, 68, 90
Sneinton	66, 72, 80
Somerset	8, 15, 22, 37, 59
South Carlton (Lincs)	5
South Leverton	22
Southwell	6, 18, 21-22, 38, 66-74, 76, 89
Spalding	6, 13, 19, 53-57, 59-63, 79-80
Spilsby	54-55, 58, 60-63
Spridlington	68
Staffordshire	56, 79, 81, 84
Stamford	6, 10, 30, 53-54, 57-64, 90
Stanford on Soar	85
Staunton	87
Sturton le Steeple	5, 22
Styrrup	69
Suffolk	57, 59, 61, 71
Surrey	58, 83
Sussex	38
Sutton Bonington	84, 85
Sutton Bridge	62
Sutton in Ashfield	68
Sutton on Trent	5-6, 8, 11, 15-17, 22, 25, 43-45, 61, 76-77, 87-88, 90
Swineshead	54, 59
Tattershall	6
Thorpe	22, 68, 71, 72
Thorpe St Peter	57
Tollerton	71
Torksey	5
Toton	9, 22
Toynton	58
Upton (Southwell)	22, 74
USA	16, 40, 87
Waddington	68
Warsop	66-68, 70-72, 75
Warwickshire	56, 60, 61, 80-81
Washingborough	57
Wellow	72
West Bridgford	76
West Burton	22
West Leake	38, 66, 84-86, 90-91
Wilford	66, 70-73
Willoughby (Lincs)	68
Willoughby (Notts)	70
Wiltshire	57
Woodborough	74
Woolsthorpe	63
Worcestershire	83
Worksop	5, 58, 60, 66-68, 71-74, 79
Wysall	85,
Yorkshire	5-6, 9, 56-61, 68-71, 73, 79, 81-82, 87, 89

Acknowledgements and Basket making Resources

Acknowledgements-

To Rupert Vinnicombe, Principal Librarian, East Nottinghamshire and David Start, Director, Heritage Lincolnshire who both encouraged and guided me through with 'A Basketful' to publication.

The Staff of Grantham, Lincoln, Newark and Nottingham Local Studies Libraries, also the Museum of Lincolnshire Life, Museum of Nottingham Life – Brewhouse Yard and Grantham and Retford Museums. Thanks also to the staff of Lincolnshire and Nottinghamshire Archives.

To Trevor Jones for professionally scanning the images, the Summers family, John Marshall and in alphabetical order - Beckingham LHS, Mrs Ros Boyce (Lincolnshire Illustrations Index), Mrs P. Butt, East Leake & District LHS, Mrs A. Elmore, Michael Elsden, Mrs Marjorie Ford, Corinne Fawcett, Terry Fry, Tony Grundy, Bernard Heathcote, David Hopkins, Mrs Irene Higgs, Mrs B. Mills, Mrs F. Moore, Mr J.R. Pinchbeck, Mrs F. Proudley, Mrs B. Robinson, Miss R. Tinley, Mrs F. Waters, the Walker family of Elston and Cyril Wakefield.

Basket making Resources.

Archives-
Nottinghamshire Archives, County House, Castle Meadow Road, Nottm NG2 1AG archives@nottscc.gov.uk
Lincolnshire Archives, St Rumbold Street, Lincoln, LN2 5AB, www.lincolnshire.gov.uk/archives

Libraries – Local Studies and Photographic Collections
Nottingham Central Library, Angel Row, Nottingham, NG1 6HP
Newark Library, Beaumond Gardens, Balderton Gate, Newark, NG24 1UW
Lincoln Central Library, Free School Lane, Lincoln LN2 1EZ
Grantham Library, Isaac Newton Centre, Grantham, NG31 6EE
Grimsby Central Library, (Hallgarth Photographic Collection), Town Hall Square, Grimsby, DN31 1HG
Nottinghamshire – www.picturethepast.org.uk
Lincolnshire – illustrations_index@lincolnshire.gov.uk

Museums-
Bassetlaw Museum (Welchman Photographic Collection), Amcott House, 40 Grove Street, Retford. DN22 6LD
Grantham, St Peters Hill, Grantham NG31 6PY
Museum of Lincolnshire Life, Burton Road, Lincoln, LN1 3LY
Newark Resource Centre via Millgate Museum, Newark, NG24 4TS Brunel Drive, Newark
Museum of Nottingham Life, Brewhouse Yard, Castle Boulevard, Nottingham, NG7 1FB

The Basketmakers' Association
www.basketassoc.org

Willow in the 21st century

The future could be 'Green' with biomass willow

SRC – Short Rotation Coppice is a financially viable and low risk crop, and an alternative to traditional arable crops. Willow varieties for SRC were trialed in Sweden, a world leader with 25% of its energy needs via biomass. The UK Government has set a national target of obtaining 20% of its electricity supply from renewable sources by the year 2020.

Growing crops for energy, from home central heating to a power station is becoming a reality, thanks to Trent Valley willows. At Cottam and West Burton, biomass willow is fired with coal to reduce carbon emissions. Drax Power Station aims for 10% of its electricity from biomass by 2010. Dunham on Trent School's heating system is also fueled by biomass from willow grown in the school grounds.

So although willow for basketry is in serious decline locally, it has emerged a fuel of the future. Indeed the biggest grower of biomass willow in the UK is Nottinghamshire farmer, John Strawson with over 200 hectares. In 2001 he established Renewable Energy Growers Ltd, representing 80% of the country's growers.

By using biomass and helping reduce global warming from carbon emissions, the future could indeed be 'greener', thanks to willow.

Willow as a landscape feature

As seen on television and at the Chelsea Flower Show, willow is in fashion for gardening and landscape projects, with domes, tunnels, fedges and garden furniture made with living willow.

A number of local schools have living willow structures including North Muskham, and Beckingham, with Long Bennington having a large 'green' caterpillar to enjoy. Rushcliffe and Rufford Country Parks also have willow structures and have both run willow workshops.

Willow preserved at the Farndon Willow Holt.

Although originally a basketry willow holt, it had a number of other willow species added by local willow experts and botanists, Mr and Mrs Leiver Howitt. Following their deaths, the Nottinghamshire Wildlife Trust purchased the overgrown Holt in 1986, and after a comprehensive survey, set about its restoration with the support of the Brackenhurst Campus of Trent University and the Farndon Residents Environmental Group.

After ten years and a generous grant from WREN (Waste Recycling Environment Ltd) the 10 hectare site has had extensive replanting and the ambitious project is nearing completion.

The Willow Works and Beckingham Marshes

Grants from the National Lottery Heritage Fund and the Nationwide Building Society have enabled an exciting project to proceed involving a 488 hectare site known as 'Beckingham Marshes'. The project has already preserved the former Willow Works (see page 24), a rare surviving purpose built building of this once nationally important willow growing area. The marshes were formerly a rich wet grassland with a number of willow holts, but were extensively drained during the 1960s.

The present owners, the Environment Agency, plan to re-establish the wet habitat once again, working with the tenant farmers and the Royal Society for the Protection of Birds, supported by the Parish Council and the Local History Society. The project when completed will provide the largest inland wetland area in the country and a very welcome facility no doubt to birds and wildlife generally, but also the public and hopefully basketry willows.

Rod Peelers

This beautiful photograph was taken by Newark photographer Frank Robinson about 1900, in the grounds of Horace Mills Works, on Farndon Road, Newark.

The elderly couple portray an idyllic rustic scene, but the reality was the need to earn with a seasonable job.

The photograph was rescued from the first floor of some outbuildings following heavy snow and roof collapse. Papers emerged beneath the snow, ice and pantile fragments, and the photograph without a blemish. A miraculous survival.

Nottinghamshire County Council

Heritage Lincolnshire

In partnership with Lincolnshire County Council